Walk the High Wire

Award-winning entries
from the 1994
W H Smith
Young Writers' Competition

MACMILLAN
CHILDREN'S BOOKS

First published 1995 by Macmillan Children's Books

a division of Macmillan Publishers Limited
Cavaye Place London SW10 9PG
and Basingstoke

Associated companies throughout the world

ISBN 0 333 62755 5

1 3 5 7 9 8 6 4 2

A CIP catalogue record for this book is available from the British Library.

Phototypeset by Intype, London
Printed by Cox & Wyman Ltd, Reading

Contents

INTRODUCTION

One of the perks of being Chairman of W H Smith is that each April, when the new *Young Writers' Competition* anthology is published, I am given my own copy. This is always something to look forward to. Each year brings new discoveries: an idea or an attitude which makes me think hard; a reminiscence which draws me back to my own childhood, or makes me watch my own children with still greater fascination; an arresting phrase and new names which I know are ones to watch.

The competition has been running annually since 1959. We keep a complete record of all winners and runners-up for every one of those thirty-six years. We regularly go through this archive to see if we recognize any famous or emerging names, people who now earn their living by writing or in a related discipline. Each year we find another person to add to the list.

Neil Bartlett is such a discovery. Neil won a prize on two separate occasions, once in 1967 as an exuberant primary school writer, and again in 1975 as an altogether more sobre poet. Now, as founder of the production company *Gloria*, writer and translator of several stage plays, and, most recently as Artistic Director of the Lyric Theatre, Hammersmith, Neil can look back on his early success and assess the effect of winning those prizes:

"When I was at school, reading and writing was my great escape route – into other worlds, other futures, into my own mind. By reading I learnt about other people's voices: by writing, I learnt about my own. There's nothing like putting your own voice down in black and white on paper, to give you a sense of yourself, of what you think, what you feel, what you want.

"The W H Smith Young Writers' Competition is based on one simple fine and very good idea: that all young people can and should write for themselves and about themselves, that's the important thing."

I like Neil's description of writing as an escape route. Are we sometimes in danger of forgetting just how powerful an experience writing can be? We're very quick to say how *important* it is (by which we mean for passing examinations and getting jobs) – but exciting? transforming? revelatory?

Yet I guarantee that if you read the work in this book, at least one piece will strike a chord, absorb or amaze you – and you will forget that it is written by a young, inexperienced writer and be drawn into the energy and conviction of the narrative. That is the excitement which the judges seek (and always find), and which we all celebrate.

There is a tradition of thanking parents and teachers in this introduction, and it would be unthinkable to break with it. Year after year parents and teachers create the environment in which keen readers and writers flourish; they read, listen to and discuss new work in all its stages with the young writers. And while we always say thank you, we cannot escape the fact that our gratitude is tucked away in this introduction. Later in a writer's career, some lucky parents and teachers may be mentioned in a dedication – once again, peripheral to the main body of the book. So, it was with particular pleasure that the judges this year found Zoë Brigley's poem, *My Mum, the poetry magician.* She celebrates her mother's passion for books which has meant that Zoë has *lived* each story and poem:

> "I was there when the Highwayman
> Met his grizzly end,
> When the Ancient Mariner
> Was telling the story . . ."

and this leads inevitably to the conclusion of her poem:

> "She gave me the confidence
> To walk the high wire."

As you can see, this gave *us* the title for this book and puts parents, at least, both on the cover and in the main body of the book itself.

There was a record number of entries to the competition in 1994 – a total of 33,000, which is the highest entry in over ten years. We were delighted and so, too, were the judges, for despite the increased workload they all commented on the very high standard of the work they read and said how much they had enjoyed it. This gives the lie to the gloomiest predictions of mass illiteracy which we seem to read almost daily in the newspapers and hear on television.

Since we know what an unstable career writing can be, it was reassuring to see other interests in evidence in the writing in this year's book. Among other possible alternative professions, I noticed a musician and a fireman. But I was particularly struck by Jane Cassidy – I had never met anyone who wanted to be a traffic warden until I met Jane this summer at the prize-giving. Even in this apparently narrow career, however, she intends to exercise her imagination – she "might even paint some more double yellow lines beside parked cars when nobody was looking and give out more parking tickets." I feel confident that all the writers in this book will bring the same determination, dedication and creativity to their chosen professions, whatever they might be.

Jeremy Hardie
Chairman of the W H Smith Group

Advisory panel of judges: Ted Hughes (Chairman), Michael Baldwin, Edward Blishen, Andrew Davies, Janni Howker, Jan Mark and Kit Wright.

Preliminary panel of judges: Lynn Barclay, Charlotte Brook Smith, Richard Brookfield, Linda Hoare, Anna Hopewell, Barry Maybury, Richard Quarshie, Timothy Rogers, Betty Rosen, Professor Harold Rosen, Sheila Shannon and Anthony Weeks-Pearson.

UNLOOKED-FOR COMPANIONS FOR THE NEW JOURNEY

Rachel de Benedicitis (14)

Emma Morning (16)

*In the Beginning . . .

In the beginning was the . . . word, obedience and I, the chosen one, ready for an easy life. Pampered in paradise. Made from a rib. Complete and ready. New beginnings. Birds of the air and beasts of the field. Mint, new and fresh. The buffalo, the lion, the lambs. Names coming into my head, put there by him and Him.

In the beginning was the . . . relationship. Man and woman. Flesh of his flesh. Body naked, but not ashamed. Open and honest, with no sin, not even curiosity. Innocents. I worked with him as a help-mate, and tasted the fruits, and loved, honoured and obeyed, as anyone would, not wishing to drink or fend for themselves.

In the beginning was the . . . choice. Good and evil. Dark and light, and the first glimmering of independence. Me from him, and me from Him. To obey, or to go one's own way and look for enlightenment. One flesh, but two, separate thoughts.

In the beginning was . . . a serpent. New thoughts in my head, feelings . . . put there by him, and not Him. Thoughts of curiosity. A need to know. A need to experience and to have my own emotions, not just his, or His. An escape from bland perfection to taste sweet and sour, salt and sugar, the new forbidden fruits.

In the beginning was . . . a tree. Tall, straight and set apart. A fence just asking to be climbed. A wall just waiting to be removed, a boundary to be crossed, a curtain to be drawn back. Fruit, disappointing at first, but an acquired taste. Heady like wine. Exhilarating like rain on a summer's day.

In the beginning was . . . a separation. A fall from grace and the end of a way of life. Irritation, shame, embarrassment. Unlooked-for companions for the new journey. Yet within me, there were my own separate secrets, private thoughts and feelings – without him or Him knowing.

In the beginning . . . was a whole new beginning.

Alex McRae (14)

*The Baby

My performer sleeps:
Brown and round as a belly,
Damp as a puppy,
Spiky headed,
Watching with pink ears.
He knows his cue.
Experienced in his trade,
He mews as only a proper baby can.
After a bath, he's sodden and smiling
And screams professionally when relations come to tea.
In his plastic theatre,
The powder is Johnsons.
The greasepaint is Vaseline.

After the show, he sleeps;
But when they've gone,
Then the house is deep and breathes;
A huge whale, swimming far below,
It's the only one who knows
How special you are when you sleep.

Elizabeth Holden (8)

*Fairytale News

Today Jack climbed a beanstalk and he saw a giant at
the top and he ran back down screaming with terror.

Cinderella went to a ball and lost her big toe.
The prince threatened that if she didn't find it, he
would give her a kiss. (But she did find it. Phew!)

Hansel and Gretel starved in a wood and died.

Jack Sprat ate his fat and thought it tasted
rather nice. So he ended up eating three bowls of fat for
breakfast, four bowls of fat for lunch and five bowls of
fat for tea. (A must say that he did get a bit fat
'imself!)

The dwarfs tried to kill Snow White. Unfortunately,
Dopey fell in love with her, so it meant that Dopey
followed her around. Good news, because a prince came to
take her away, but Snow White was polite and the prince
didn't bother. The prince came all that way to see a
pretty, sweet, polite goody-two-shoes.

Well, that's all for today.

Hope you've enjoyed it.

Can you wish, just for me,
that Jack Sprat doesn't burst
eating the FAT?

Goodbye.

Barnaby Crush (7)

Nicholas Curtis

He liked everything to be how he wanted. He liked to crack jokes and play tricks on people. He had wild ideas which he always forgot about. He was very helpful but if you made a joke about him he would hate you. But after a while he would like you again. He loved to play games as long as he could be the main part or the super hero. He always seemed to get bored of things. He was a good friend. He liked *Sonic the Hedgehog*. He often changed his mind and sometimes he couldn't make up his mind in the first place. He liked football and he supported Liverpool. He was brilliant at football. He was a very fast runner and he was very very strong. He often had fights at school. He had loads of friends. He would normally find somebody to play with or if not he would play on his own. Me and Nick often found ourselves in trouble like having about six people coming after us. We often played *Sonic* and I was always being a made-up character called Wilfred the Lizard. When me and Stephen challenged Nick he would always find some excuse. He often forgot things like money or slips. He could swim pretty well. His favourite colour was red. His favourite book was *Stay Sonic*. He liked films and mega-drives. He liked animals a lot. He never ever brought any plimsolls for P.E. I remember going with him to find some school plimsolls. He used to fight over one pair of twelves. I remember one morning when I was walking to school, him coming along with these really baggy shorts. He was the best friend I've ever had and he always will be.

James Cahill (8)

*Mr Archret

There was once a man called Mr Archret. Mr Archret was the best, most well-known man in the world. He was aged a hundred and four but looked nothing like it. This was because long ago, in his seventies, he had found a powder-like substance in the grounds of Egypt and had found that the powder was well and truly magic. It kept him looking young: his hair was still brown and he didn't have any wrinkles. To make him look like this he had had to pour the powder-like stuff over him and shout, "Keep me young and never let me die." It gave him amazing stamina.

Mr Archret had two most trusted and faithful companions who were called Mr James Mince and Mr Tom Each, both in their late forties. They too had been given the powder which Mr Archret called "magic dust". They too looked much younger than they were. They all worked in the best café in the world.

Mr Archret, Mr Mince and Mr Each were all very happy except for one thing – Mr Archret had a deadly enemy. She wanted to take his place in being the best person in the world. She hated him. She was known as Old Grumpy. She had short curly hair, a dark brown dress and a white pinafore.

Apart from Old Grumpy, Mr Archret had another enemy. He was a friend of Old Grumpy and was rather stupid. He was tall and thin, with a big baggy suit. Over this he wore a very dirty cloak. He wore thick-framed glasses which were too small for him. On his head he wore a black leather hat. He and Old Grumpy lived on the streets, moving from place to place.

However, Mr Archret, Mr Mince and Mr Each all lived

in a huge house, sitting in the heart of the country. It was five times the size of a normal house. Mr Archret, Mr Mince and Mr Each all owned their own country cottage. But Mr Archret's favourite house was in Cambridge. It was the biggest of all his houses.

The Building of the Café

When they first met, Mr Archret, Mr Mince and Mr Each all needed a job to do. If you remember, they ran a café, which like Mr Archret, was world-famous. This is a story of how the café first started.

"Let's have something like a coffee or sandwich bar," suggested Mr Mince.

"No!" shouted Mr Archret. "We want to get more money than ten pounds a day!"

"Instead of a coffee bar we could have something like it," said Mr Each.

"Yes!" exclaimed Mr Archret. "Perhaps a café or restaurant!" They decided that they could build a café. They started work. The café would consist of three million bricks. They ordered one hundred tables, one hundred tablecloths and five hundred chairs. Mr Archret phoned up a place called Homecare which was a group of builders. The builders helped Mr Mince and Mr Each with the work. Mr Archret gave orders like, "Hurry up!" or "You've missed that bit out." In five months, half of the café was made. In another five months the café was finished. There were reports about it all over the world in newspapers and on television. The café was only a week old and already the best in the world.

The Robbery

Mr Archret was very proud of his silver Volvo. It was washed twice a week. Once when he was washing it, Old Grumpy walked up. She took a glance at the car, then she walked on.

That night in the bath, Mr Archret heard a funny noise. In the morning when Mr Archret was coming outside to water the flowers, he noticed his car was gone. He dashed inside.

"Mr Mince," he said, "where is my car?"

"Your what?" said Mr Mince.

"My car!"

"Oh dear," said Mr Mince, "let's go and have a look."

"Yes," murmured Mr Mince, "your car is gone. It must have been stolen."

"And I remember that Old Grumpy walked up and looked at my car," said Mr Archret. "It all means that Old Grumpy has stolen it."

"Wait," said Mr Mince, "what you are saying is that Old Grumpy looked at your car and then stole it."

"No, no," shouted Mr Archret, "*yesterday* Old Grumpy looked at my car and *last night* she stole it."

Mr Archret phoned the police.

"Hello," he said, "It's Mr Archret here, you know, yes the best in the world. Well my car's been stolen, hurry, good-bye!"

"Mr Archret," scolded Mr Mince, "you must tell the police where we are or they won't know where to come." Mr Mince told the police where they were.

In ten minutes the police were interviewing Mr Mince while Mr Archret was looking out of the window. Just then he saw a car very like his own racing down the road. Inside he saw Old Grumpy and someone else. He picked up a lovely big flagstone on the window-sill. Then he threw it at the window and broke it. SMASH! He made the hole a bit bigger and then jumped through it. He climbed into the open police car. He turned the key and he was off. He drove very fast after his own car which was the one in front of the one in front of himself. Mr Archret sped down the road and managed to get behind Old Grumpy. At the traffic lights Old

Grumpy stopped. Mr Archret rammed into the back of her. Then he got out.

"Hand over my car," he said. As he did this he held out his revolver. He was standing outside his car. Old Grumpy took out her revolver too. In the back of the car sat Mr Potter armed with a mallet.

"Get into the car," demanded Old Grumpy. Mr Archret stepped in. "You stupid woman," he said to Old Grumpy. "You will get caught when Mr Mince comes." Just then Mr Mince did come. He and the policeman both had a pair of handcuffs and a gun. Old Grumpy and Mr Potter were taken to jail and Mr Archret was given back his car.

The Pig Raid

Mr Smith, an enemy of Mr Archret was in the café. He ordered a cold salad. It cost three pounds fifty but Mr Smith thought that this was far too much and told Mr Archret that he thought that it was the worst café in the world. In anger, Mr Archret hit him around the head with a pepper mill and sent him away.

"Mr Archret," said Mr Mince, "you must never send customers away, even if you don't like them." In anger, Mr Mince forgot to shut the café properly at the end of the day. Over the road from the café was a pig farm. A pig farm is a field full of pigs. In the morning Mr Archret opened the door of the café and got the fright of his life. There were about thirty pigs eating up the contents of the fridge, which lay all over the floor.

"Mr Mince!" he shouted. Mr Mince entered the café seeing that he had left the door unlocked. "What is this?"

As well as the food there were upturned chairs, shattered wine bottles, a great big crack in the counter, a running tap and a torn tea-cloth.

"The p-pig farm gate must have b-been l-left open," stammered Mr Mince.

"That's it!" shouted Mr Archret. "I'm phoning Farmer Jones." (Mr Jones was the owner of the pig farm.) "Hello, yes, Mr Archret here. YOUR PIGS HAVE RAIDED MY CAFÉ, WHAT ARE YOU GOING TO DO? YES, I KNOW, YOU HAD BETTER PAY FOR THE DAMAGE!" And with that Mr Archret slammed the phone down. Now Mr Archret and Mr Mince always shut the café properly and Mr Each has made some pig alarms just in case.

Trouble With Mr Potter

Old Grumpy had a plan. She and Mr Potter were going to dress up as nice people and pretend to be friends with Mr Archret, Mr Mince and Mr Each. Then they were going to attack them one day, when they were talking to Mr Archret. They dressed up and went along to the café. Mr Archret, Mr Mince and Mr Each were all there. They walked up to the counter.

"Hello," chirped Old Grumpy, "we like you." Mr Archret wasn't stupid. He knew it was Old Grumpy and Mr Potter. He sent them out. But Mr Potter was very stupid and thought that Old Grumpy had told him to be nice to Mr Archret, Mr Mince and Mr Each for ever.

"Hello," he said to them as he entered alone the next day, "I like you and want to be your friend, I dislike Old Grumpy."

"Go away," ordered Mr Each, "we don't like you."

It took a week before Mr Potter was friends with Mr Archret, Mr Mince and Mr Each. Now Old Grumpy was on her own for ever.

Jessie Binns (16)

**The Sparrow in the Engine

The weeks of drills,
The hours spent sweating
Aching our brains, until
It comes
Suddenly and beautifully
It clicks, like a piece into a jigsaw,
The piece was built up, bit by bit.

At the first run-through
We thought it was good.
We built it, complete in quarter of an hour.
But it was only a sketch, and
To prove it, he took it to bits,
Again and again.
Repeating one bar, a phrase, until
The entries were like pistons.
The notes on the paper translate
To fingers on keys
Like Automaton, like machines – this
Was not our creation, we merely passed it on.

So now the puzzle is nearly complete;
Difficult runs we would have made up
(or missed out) jab out, now correct.
We are parts of an engine,
Our individuality has been painfully
Meshed into one.
But it's good.
The colours swell without thinking
The notes clash forth, billowing up like a cloud
From some incredible nuclear explosion.
The sound is big,
Really big,
And unstoppable . . .

And suddenly our conductor looks
Very old, very tired.
His little hands stop their waving
That used to command us.
He lets us get on with it
As he scrabbles around on the floor
For his score
That he's knocked off his stand.
Like a madman,
Or a sparrow,
Fluttering on the ground.

Zoë Brigley (13)

*Rachel's Bag

Out of the blue, tidy bag,
Come the school books
Regimented like soldiers.
Then the pencil-case,
With not a speck of dust
Upon its black parallel lines.
The straight zip
Growls open,
And the pencils and pens,
All in working order,
March out.
Next are the pockets,
Personally organized,
All clean and spotless.
But at the bottom of the bag,
Hidden in a forgotten corner,
Are the gloves –
The rebelling squaddies,
Who spoil the ranks
Of the sergeant mistress.

Jane Cassidy (8)

*A Traffic Warden for the Day

I would like to be a traffic warden for the day and give out big parking fines to all my friends. I would wear a black skirt, a black jacket and have a hat with a badge. I might even paint some more double yellow lines beside parked cars when nobody was looking and give out more parking tickets. When I showed my boss, he or she would be very pleased with me. I would get up early to try and catch lorries and vans unloading stock for the shops. I would catch people out who were parked on double yellow lines where people didn't expect me and I would give them an even bigger fine. I would take my lunch in my bag so I wouldn't miss any duty. I might like to be a traffic warden for a day but I might get sick of it and I can tell you I would be glad to put my feet up and turn on the TV.

John Finnemore (17)

*Shopping at Mog's

The brass cowbell stood on the left-hand side of the dusty grey step. This meant, for those in the know, that Mog was out "erranding". I edged past the battered bell which squatted on the step, leering up at me with its crudely painted pixie face. Painting was a passion with Mog, not landscapes on canvas, but contorted faces and features on all manner of objects. Into the back garden, where, by the murky fishpond, stood a lopsided earthenware swan, staring out a grinning

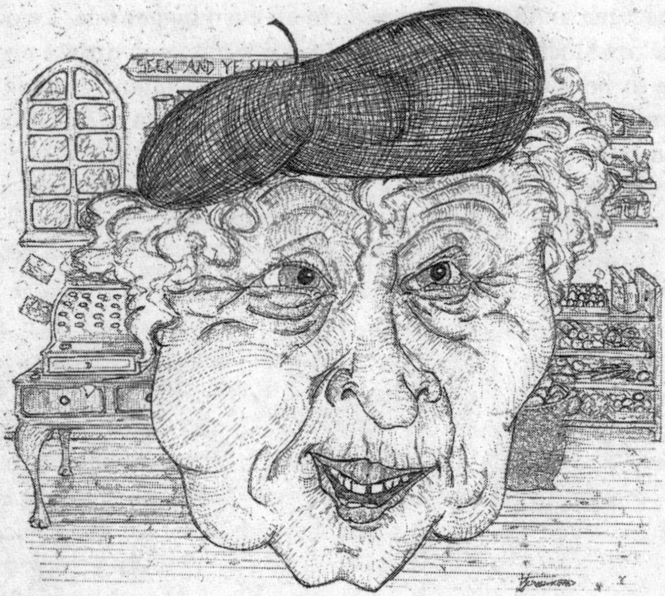

John Finnemore (17)

gnome on the other side. I picked up the swan, and upturned her to reveal the coin-sized hole left by the potter. A brief shake, painted neck blurring into a block of fuzzy white, and the rusty key she guarded clattered out of the hole, on to the mossy path below.

I returned to the shop, and graunched the key through a protesting semicircle inside the lock. The door still refused to open, guarding the shop in its mistress's absence. But I knew the trick. I held down the handle with one hand and, with the other, dealt the top of the door a sharp blow near the hinge. The warped wood that had held the door back juddered past the frame, and the shop reluctantly admitted me.

I flicked the plastic card from "Closed" to "Open". Once, the larger sponsored sign had proclaimed "Closed – Even For The Sale Of Watney's!" – but Mog, wielding a pair of sharp scissors, had soon put a stop to that. I walked round the little shop, pulling up the thick, black blinds to let the watery yellow spring sunshine stream in, high-lighting every tiny speck of dust as they bobbed in battalions about the room.

I stepped back into the yard to collect the twisted brush from its shady resting place, and almost collided with Mog, trotting up the path like a multi-coloured magpie. She wore an orange mac, which flapped over her purple cardigan and long tweedy skirt like a half-discarded skin. On her head she wore an aggressively green beret, drunkenly lolling on her startlingly white hair. Her face was a landscape of pucks and wrinkles, surrounding her features like ripples around stones thrown in a pool. The staccato pecks that inevitably accompanied her were made by a pair of ancient, black, wooden shoes, each painted with one of Mog's lecherous faces. She pulled up abruptly, and squinted up at me, head on one side and eyes screwed up in effort. Too proud to wear glasses, even at seventy-nine ("You wouldn't catch my

Mother wearing specs, nor my Grandmother, NOR none of my Aunties!") this was a daily routine.

"It's only me, Mog . . ."

"I can see quite well who you are, boy," she said, using her most correct speech, "I was MERELY wondering what you think you're doing standing in the yard, gawping like a lemon!"

A woman born to speak in capitals, Mog was always piqued at the suggestion that her eyesight was not what her female relations would have expected.

"If you 'ave QUATE finished smirking, you can go and tidy the shop up: I'm Expecting A Customer at nine-fifteen." She swept into the garden, green beret perched above her orange mac like the stalk on a carrot. With Mog, visitors to the shop were divided into two groups: Customers only came by prior appointment and were a very select bunch of village worthies; Shoppers wandered in off the street, and could all too easily be members of the sinister band of the Government's black-hand gang, Her Majesty's Inspectorate.

Inside the shop it was cool, and there was the familiar smell of potatoes, varnish and apples. The groaning old writing desk Mog used as her counter, cash register and safe sat tiredly at the far end of the shop, with shelves jumbled with goods radiating from it along the walls. Mog had never worked out a system for storing goods: her motto, hand painted over the window, was "Seek and ye shall find". As I swept the warped, wooden floor, pieces of the old, perished varnish were flicked off the floor by my brush and sent spinning off into the air to dance with the dust gyrating in the sunlight.

Through the frosted window, I could see Mog clattering up the crazy paving, laden down with two cauliflowers and a tray of eggs. As she reached the door, the clattering stopped, and she let out an imperious whistle. I crossed to the door and opened it, bowing low in mock servility. Gathering an imaginary ball grown around her, she minced into the room in her elaborate imitation of landed gentry. I held out my hand for a tip, and she responded by pressing a cauliflower into it.

"Lady Morgana Venables-Venables-Smythe presents 'er 'ighly esteemed compliments, and begs to hinquire when 'is bone-idleness the lay-about is going to get some work done?"

"Your wish is my command, your crochetyness." I began an exaggerated butler's hobble to the discarded broom, but was brought up short by another most unladylike whistle.

"Come and take these eggs, if you want to be useful. The ones on the right are Rosie's, they're worth about . . . twelve pence each, the left ones are from Martha, so only nine pence, as usual, and the white ones are Brenda's – at least fifteen pence for hers."

Most people sell eggs by size or colour; only Mog sold them by chicken. Again, I turned to the rack of eggs and again, I was arrested by a noise. Footsteps were tramping up the path. Mog, flabbergasted, scooted to the window and squinted out.

"SURELY it's not My Customer! It's FAR too early. My Customers are never so rude . . . It must be a Shopper . . . come over here boy, I can't see a THING in this sun."

I ran over to the window, and peered out. A tall man, dressed rather self-consciously in holiday clothes, was picking his way up the path. It was obvious that he would be far more at home in a retiring blue suit, but it was not to be. He was on holiday and determined to holiday properly. I knew, with a sinking heart, that Mog would immediately identify him as a heathen shop inspector, scum of the earth. I relayed the unhappy news to Mog.

"It's a Shopper . . . A holiday shopper I'm afraid."

"No! He'll be here when My Customer arrives! Has the

man no manners?" wailed Mog, taking logic by the hair, and giving it a vicious twist. "Right, get away from the door and get rid of him as soon as possible. If 'e stays, I'll be another customer, and stand be 'ind 'im and tut. Jus' get rid of 'im before My Customer arrives!"

We took up our positions in the shop, and stood by to repel boarders.

The shopper passed the window, and we heard his soft, shambling footsteps trudging up the crazy paving. The shuffling stopped, and the handle of the door was grated round. Then we heard the thud of an uninitiated shopper trying to push the door open. There was a pause. In my mind's eye I could see the shopper bending down ponderously to peer through the crack of the door, looking for the lock. Again the graunching. I turned to look at Mog. She was leaning forward towards the door, eyes screwed up as if to try and gaze through the door at the intruder hell-bent on spending his money at her shop. Thud! Mog's face lit up. The shopper had fallen at the first hurdle, and would be back to his little square of sand, fenced in with windbreaks, beach bags and sticky-faced small children, before the Customer was within sniffing distance of the shop. There was a rap at the window. Mog whipped round as if shot. Twenty lugubrious faces of the so nearly thwarted shopper peered through the frosted glass. Mog gave a little squeal of annoyance. I went to open the door.

The shopper was a tall man, surrounded by a little haze of late spring sunshine, sand and tiredness. Sand seemed to cling to every ledge of him, in his clothes, his limp hair; there even seemed to be sand in the wrinkles of his face. He wore the sand with a baffled weariness, as something irritating but immovable, an inevitable consequence of having strayed within fifty miles of the coast. I tried to imagine him sandless, in a suit and a comfortable office. I had a sneaking suspicion that as soon as his car slid back into the city, the sand would disappear, and he would immediately be coated in dust. He murmured a greeting to me and slunk into the coolness of the shop. He walked with a stoop, but it was less the stoop of a man with a back problem than the stoop of a man who often walks into the top of door-frames. Mog was lurking by a barrel of apples, buzzing angrily. The Sandman seemed a little taken aback by the malevolent jumble of colours in front of him. He made an odd little sighing noise with his cheeks, rather like a horse with a cold, and turned to inspect the rows of vegetables. His hopeless languor stirred Mog into desperation. She pattered her way to the adjacent display, and began her "tutting". This is a poor description of the barrage of clicking Mog could produce from her tongue and palate, designed to convey the just impatience of one shopper at the criminal slowness of another. The effect it produced in the Sandman was similar to that of a sleeping bloodhound that has just had its tail pulled. An eloquent hopelessness and defeat sprang into his sand-encrusted eyes. In addition to magnetic sand particles, a vicious fate had put him in the same shop as a woman who clicked at him. He edged mournfully along to another shelf of assorted goods, and kept an apprehensive eye on Mog. Mog promptly clattered around the shelves to appear on the other side of him. She brushed a loop of white hair back under her beret, and let loose another round of clicks. The Sandman leapt back in terror. Mog matched his pace, and giving up any pretence of being a shopper, stared up into his bewildered face, and gave him a medley of her greatest clicks. The poor man looked more like a thwarted bloodhound than many bloodhounds do. I half expected him to throw back his head and howl. He turned to me in appeal, a rail against the unfairness of life, fortune, and mad women in country shops hovering on his lips, and then fled the shop, a renewed volley of clicks ringing in his ears.

A grin split Mog's face like a river, and with a cackle she scurried to the writing desk-cum-counter. Chuckling to herself, she took a postcard from a drawer, and, with a stub of crayon, drew yet another tally mark on the back of it.

Zilla Appiah-Carr (16)

The Perfect Way of Living

The six women leaned on the palm trees,
As the starlight shone around them.
There they ate their meal.

The aroma of fish drifted through the air
As they exchanged jokes
And ate gracefully with their hands.

The hot air kept them awake,
For the whole night
As they relaxed, after a busy day.

As they talked, the moon stared down on them
She was pleased to be in their midst
She wished that she could converse with them.

However, she remembered that she would have to watch the world go by
As she was only a moon.

Lucy Jack (13)

*Zimmer Kings

Granny's Bridge Partners

Crinkly, like old paper bags,
Mottled, gnarled hands,
With fingers which have been in the bath too long.

Varicose veins
Creeping up their legs like strangling ivy,
Faces like weather-beaten tarpaulin.

But there is warmth under that tarpaulin:
A glowing candle,
Revealed by a radiant smile.

Thomas Newdick (14)

Another Bus Journey

The bus cuts through the scum-covered, grey-brown puddle, splattering the *Nescafé* advert. Muddy water drips through the golden coffee granules. The carbon-stained exhaust pipe throbs rhythmically, rattling the red wheel arch panel.

I swing on to the bus through the door, my hand grasping the plastic-coated hand pole. The conductor stands at the foot of the stairs to the upper deck, fiddling noisily with his ticket machine, lurching violently as the bus pulls away, leaving a plume of dirty smoke behind it. I head through the corridor to the nearest empty seat. The dull tartan cover is impregnated with cigarette ash and semi-scraped-off chewing-gum. I fling my battered rucksack on to the opposite seat.

The bus gradually tacks through the steady stream of traffic that rumbles through the town like a mud flow. Masked cyclists throw their sturdy bikes dangerously through gaps between building firms' dusty trucks and rattling taxis with drivers straining out of their cab windows shouting to one another, though they're not far apart. Turbanned Arabs sit in the rear of misty-windowed Bentleys tapping on notepad computers, reps in sweaty polyester suits, ties loosened, quietly but urgently speak on their car phones, often running their fingers through their dull hair as the traffic halts and they gradually slow down to a standstill.

The bus's air brakes hiss and groan. The vehicle leans towards the neon shop fronts and pulls into the kerb. The student with tie-died clothing; the young man with a Walkman and loosely stitched grey jumper; an old Indian woman with a shopping bag, hooded; long-haired, tasselled, studded man grazing on polystyrene-packaged chips; an old man, grey, nameless, faceless – they all wait. The rain begins to sweep through the city, making umbrellas bloom, pedestrians run to shelter under the concrete awning of Iran Airways. The bus's windscreen wipers swing uselessly, squeaking . . . every third swing. An over-made-up woman catches her shoe on the pavement lip by a gurgling drain. The conductor glances uninterestedly at my Travelcard before moving on into the cigarette smoke. The man opposite me turns from his foreign newspaper and stares at the raindrops weaving their way down the window.

At the next stop the passengers spread their bags over the seats next to them as the damp, dripping assortment of people enter the bus shedding water along the aisle. London darkens quickly and faces on the street become just shadows, lights reflected in a multitude of puddles. A police car in another street; a digger working by floodlight at roadworks; cafés taking in the chairs and tables; Italian waiters wiping down plastic surfaces, moving salt and pepper pots six to a hand. The last couple at a table talk over cheap, weak coffee. The lights at a launderette flicker and go out. Shoppers from the department stores laden with bags of all sizes and colours, Selfridges, Fortnum and Mason, Harrods, load their expensive purchases on to the bus.

Uniformed, named, store workers get on and off, along with office workers, railworkers. Tramps leave their day haunts in the dustbin-filled back streets and sit outside a closing McDonalds. It is nearly my stop, just outside the boarded-up office block. No one else gets off the bus. I get up, swinging my pack over my shoulder, jump off the foot plate and watch the bus disappear at the end of the brightly lit street, sit down in the vandalized bus shelter, waiting for the next one to come. Another bus, another story.

IT'S ALL A BIT COMPLICATED IN OUR HOUSE

Blanche McIntyre (12)

*Being Naughty

When I am naughty,
I think of
what I am going to do.
Then laughter
bubbles up inside me.
After my body
is full up with laughter,
my bottom jaw
drops open and the laughter falls out.
Emily says,
"What are you laughing about?"
and I answer "He, he he,"
and carry on laughing.
Then I put my hand over my mouth
and run downstairs.

Charlotte Gunner (7)

Charlotte Gunner

Barney Jeffries (15)

**Danny

First of all there was the problem of where to go. My younger brother, Danny, had already made up his mind: "Danny goin to Venchur, Danny goin to Venchur," he screamed, till I locked him in the cupboard.

"Venchur" was Danny's interpretation of Adventure Village, the theme park near Canterbury, about fifteen miles away. I loved my first visit to Adventure Village, and the second time wasn't too bad either, but after eleven visits the excitement wears off somewhat. This doesn't seem to bother Danny, however. Given the chance, I think he would go to "Venchur" every day. I don't quite understand this, seeing as he spends half the time in tears. There are many things about Danny which I don't quite understand. I think most child psychiatrists would be stumped as well.

Sara, my eleven-year-old sister, suggested that we go ice skating. Sara makes me sick. She wins every race on sports day, is academically very bright, and can play the clarinet, piano and guitar in a way that would make the Pied Piper abandon his music and settle down to a career in accountancy. She has flowing blond hair and a "thousand-ship" face. Perhaps most sickening of all is the fact that she's also a *very, very nice person*. In short, she is the personification of perfection. It is frightening to think that she is my sister, and Danny's sister; proof, I think, of the uncertain nature of the genetic theory.

My mother vetoed her suggestion, saying that Danny was just too young. Last time we went ice skating Danny managed to run over four of his fingers. Not so they came right off, unfortunately, but enough to cover the whole of the rink with blood.

Mum's idea was Brammel House, a nearby stately home. "If you're good," she told the younger generation, "I'll buy you an ice-cream." Thrillsville! I hate stately homes as much as I hate Adventure Village. They are just so boring. Who wants to go and see the house of someone richer than themselves? It just makes you jealous. In my opinion they should move the rich people into council houses in Birmingham, sell all the furniture and give the money to charity, and open the places up as shelters for the homeless.

I tentatively suggested that we should go and see Chowley Town in their FA Cup match against Barnsley. Chowley had never qualified for the FA Cup third round before, but this year, thanks to a favourable draw, a 'flu epidemic and some rather dodgy refereeing decisions, they had done it. This proposal was greeted by shouts and kicks from inside the cupboard. Danny hates football, and gets bored after just a couple of minutes. Unfortunately he nearly always gets his own way. Having to do the same thing as a five-year-old is bad enough, but having to do the same thing as an immature five-year-old is pure hell. I let him out of the cupboard with a light kick.

Finally we decided to go to the beach. The five of us, plus Bradley the dog, packed into our Citroen 2CV. Even Bradley seemed to be whimpering at the prospect of a forty mile journey with Danny. I can't say I blame him.

After three and a half minutes a voice piped up from the back of the car:

"How mush furver, Mummy?"

"Not much further now dear," Mum lied, "Why don't we play 'I spy'?"

Oh no!

The holiday traffic was awful and we had to endure nearly two hours of "My pie wiv my ickle pie, somefin binnin wiv . . ." This was made worse by the fact that Danny doesn't know many letters, or words for that matter. I was relieved when we arrived at the crowded Blacksands car-park.

We had already piled out of the 2CV when Danny inquired as to the whereabouts of his spade. He was supposed to have brought it himself but had evidently forgotten.

"Couldn't you just do without your spade for one day, darling?" Mum asked pleadingly. Danny's response was obvious:

"*No no no no no no no no no!*" he yelled, jumping into the driving seat and trying to start the car.

"Daniel," snapped Dad, "What do you think you're doing?"

Danny thinking? That was a novel idea.

"Goin ome fesh Spadey."

I was honestly expecting Mum or Dad to give in and "Go ome fesh Spadey" but, surprisingly, they didn't.

"Danny," suggested Mum, "If you're good and forget about Spuddy, I . . ."

"Spadey," corrected Danny, rather put out.

"If you're good and forget about Spadey, I'll buy you an ice-cream."

"No." Danny shouted, "Want Spadey."

"An ice-cream and a packet of sweets?"

"No, want Spadey."

"An ice-cream and a packet of sweets and some crisps?"

"No, want Spadey."

"An ice-cream and a packet of sweets and some crisps and one pound extra pocket money?"

This was getting like one of those quizzes on the radio where they add another prize each time someone gets the answer wrong.

Still Danny insisted that he wanted his spade.

"An ice cream and a packet of sweets and some crisps and one pound extra pocket money and [deep breath] a trip to Adventure Village very soon?"

"OK." Danny replied coolly. Talk about bribery! He may be stupid and immature most of the time but when it comes to Mum and Dad he is smart. Most five-year-olds would have accepted the ice-cream, but our Danny knew that Mum would keep on with the offers. He plays her like a concert pianist plays a grand piano.

It was then that we realized Bradley was missing. We walked down the steep cliff path that led to the beach, calling the dog all the way. As we stepped on to the sand we were greeted by a very smug looking Bradley with the shredded remains of a beach ball in his mouth.

"Bradley, where did you get that ball?" asked my father.

Bradley said nothing, which is hardly surprising.

"You're a very bad dog," Dad told him.

Bradley ran away with his ears drooping and his tail between his legs.

We walked along the beach until we found a yard of free sand. It took a long time. I'd just set out the rug when Bradley appeared with another beach ball in his mouth. I don't think that I should write down what Dad said. Bradley soon realized that we were not pleased with him, and he quietly slunk off.

I went off for a swim. The water was freezing, but after a while I got used to it. I swam out until the noise of the beach had died away. Floating on my back it was a great relief to escape my family for a while. I wondered how we could be so different. I honestly think that I would be relieved if someone told me I was adopted. The gentle rocking of the waves had almost lulled me to sleep when I heard a shout from the beach:

"Bradley, bad dog!" Uh oh!

I swam back to shore in time to see Dad dragging Bradley along by the scruff of the neck. Next to them were the remains of yet another beach ball. Nearby, a sobbing child was being comforted by his parents, who looked daggers at our family.

"I'm taking him back to the car," Dad explained.

I went back to the camp for lunch. I'd asked for cheese and tomato sandwiches, Danny had asked for ham, but as soon as we'd got our picnic out Danny announced that he didn't like ham. I ate my sandwiches as quickly as possible, because I knew Mum would ask me to swap lunches with him.

Danny started crying and throwing his lunch everywhere. We got really evil looks from the other people on the beach. I wanted to tell them that I'm a normal person, and that I'd never seen this family before. Maybe my real family, my biological parents, were on the beach somewhere, ready to rescue their long-lost son and whisk him away to their beautiful cottage in the country . . .

Nope. My very real family were sitting three feet away from me, arguing about who'd asked for which flavour of sandwich.

After lunch Danny suddenly announced that he was hot.

"Whysit hot, Mummy?" Danny asked.

"Because it's summer, dear," Mum replied.

"Whysnot winner an Cwismas an snow?" Oh good grief, he'll be asking why we don't live on Mars next. Come to think of it, he'd probably feel at home there.

"Why don't you ask that man over there to make it Christmas for you?" I suggested, forgetting that Danny had not yet mastered the art of sarcasm.

"Oy, misser, make Cwismas for Danny."

The stony-faced old man turned and glared at us.

My skin began to prickle. "Danny!"

"Now Danny, that's very naughty," lectured Mum. "You know that you should never ask for anything without saying please."

Sara asked if she could go to the arcade on the pier. Mum and Dad don't really approve of arcade games but Sara is just so lucky at everything that they let us go.

After losing a couple of quid on the slot machines I decided to go and see how Sara was getting on. I was just in time to hear a clattering of money coming from the brightly coloured Jackpot machine where Sara was standing. The whole arcade had turned to see the lucky winner. I saw her write down the following in the back of her diary:

Accounts 4.8.93	
Fruit machine	*–10p*
" "	*+£7.50*
Penny pusher	*–2p*
" "	*+£9.48*
Fruit machine	*–10p*
" "	*+£21.00*

I congratulated her enthusiastically, though at that moment I felt like breaking her neck, and she treated me to an ice-cream. The two of us then went to find Mum, Dad and the imbecile. We met them at the bottom of the cliff. Danny was throwing another tantrum, because Dad wouldn't let him climb up the steep face. That must be a first, Danny not doing what he wants. Together we managed to drag him up the steps while Mum explained that we had decided to call in on Gran on the way home. I didn't think this was a good idea, as Gran lives very near to Adventure Village, but I didn't say anything. In the car park a rather nasty shock awaited us.

A window of the car was broken, and Bradley had gone.

Somebody had written "Dogs die in hot cars" across the windscreen in a repulsive green spray paint. Dad wiped a small tear from his eye. I felt sorry for him, as that car is, inexplicably, his pride and joy.

"Oh poor Bradley, where can he be?" sobbed Mum.

As if in answer we heard a voice over the tannoy.

"Could the owners of a Cocker spaniel who answers to the name of 'Bad Dog' please come to the Island Head Restaurant. Thank you."

Without hesitation, my mother bounded off in the direction of the restaurant, Sara close on her heels. Within a few minutes they returned, leading a smirking Bradley.

As we packed into the car and drove off we must have looked quite a sight: the six of us packed into a vandalized 2CV with "Dogs die in hot cars" sprayed across the windscreen. Thankfully Danny fell asleep after a few minutes so we were able to listen to the football on the radio. We were just in time to hear:

" *. . . and Barnsley are on the attack yet again. Futcher on the wing steals inside, shoots, and he's scored. Yes, brilliant goal. That makes it Chowley 0 Barnsley 11 . . .* "

Eleven, nil! *ELEVEN, NIL!*

"*. . . and there's the final whistle.*"

Oh dear.

We were almost at Gran's house with Danny still asleep. It had been a good journey. Then, just as we were passing Adventure Village, Bradley sat up and licked Danny's face. He woke up and immediately knew where we were.

"Danny goin to Venchur, Danny goin to Venchur," he yelled, "Mummy say so!"

If I'd been his parent I would have drop-kicked him out of the window there and then. But Mum and Dad are just too kind hearted. Or stupid.

"We have got time," says Mum.

"And money," says Dad.

"We did promise," they decide.

And so he gets his way again.

I hate him. I hate the way Mum and Dad spoil him. I hate Sara for being so damn good at everything. I hate whoever defaced our car. I hate the Chowley defence. And I'm not too keen on their attack either. I hate Barnsley. I hate Blacksands beach. I hate Adventure Village even more. I hate stately homes.

And I guess I hate myself a little bit too.

Catherine Jones (17)

Sarah Nelson (14)

*My Sister

My sister is a face I recognize but do not know,
The owner of a green toothbrush,
A lover of hairspray, but I do not know which brand.
She owns the room next door to me
But has lost the key and will not try to find it.
She is the builder of a wall I cannot knock down.
She is a book and I am blind.
I am music and she is deaf.
She is water dripping away
That I desperately want to hold before it is gone.
She is a stranger I am longing to meet,
But whom I fear I never shall.
I am a box she does not want to open.
I am a prayer she does not want to answer.
Will not answer. Cannot answer?
I am a sandtimer running out of time.

Eleanor Franks (14)

Flesh and Blood

Today is Wednesday. The Easter holidays began yesterday. In the larder are two Easter eggs and seven Creme Eggs.

My parents are at work for another two weeks and my older sister is on work experience at the Junction. She swept out this morning in her Levi's and a skinny rib, leaving a cloud of cherry perfume behind.

I pretended to be asleep when my mother went out. She knew I wasn't, but she didn't say anything. They have left the breakfast stuff out downstairs, so I finally get up and go down. There is a note on the work surface but I throw it away without reading it.

There is nothing to do, so I watch daytime television all day and bite my nails.

My mother arrives home at five, so I go upstairs. My sister returns soon after and I hear them talking animatedly downstairs. They call me to have some tea, but I ignore them.

They try to talk to me over dinner, but I stare down at my plate and pretend to feel sick. Eventually my mother gives up and turns her attention to persuading my sister to eat more. Martha is on a diet. Not that she's fat. I eat four pieces of oven ready pizza, and am still hungry. My mother frowns when I tell her this.

She is mentally comparing me to Martha, tall and thin with wavy brown hair. I make myself five rounds of jam sandwiches, and take them up to my room so that she does not see.

I go to bed early and lie awake listening to them laughing downstairs.

*

Ellen Parker (14)

Thursday is very cold. My mother makes me get up before she leaves. She wants me to do something today, she decides. I say that I will go to the library. Satisfied, she hurries out. I make myself seven pieces of buttered toast and get my chocolate out of the larder. I feel slightly sick, but will feel better if I eat. I finish half of the Creme Eggs and most of an Easter egg. I put my dungarees on and lock up the house. Martha was disdainful when she first saw them. She said they made me look like a tent. Now she has acknowledged the necessity of covering myself up.

I get my bike out and put a bag of apples in the basket. I do not feel like going into town so I head down by the river for the children's playground. I sit on one of the benches and eat an apple. A man is welding in one of the houseboats on the river. I smile at him.

It begins to rain so I get on my bike and cycle along fast-emptying streets as it begins to rain harder and harder. In the end I find shelter on the station platform. When I was younger I used to be fascinated by the station, used to love watching the trains arrive and depart for, I imagined, far-off lands. I am seized by a sudden childish urge to leave my bike and get on a train. To Ipswich, perhaps. I used to have a friend who lived on the Ipswich line.

But there is no train for two hours, so I leave the long, windy platform for the warm foyer, and from there I go out into the cold and head for the railway bridge. I have never been over it before, and I push my bike slowly up, along and then down. As I near the end I look back at the station platform. A train has just arrived and the mid-morning travellers are swarming off. I reach the end and turn around. As I return, two boys pass, very fast, on mountain bikes. There are security cameras and small screens along the length of the bridge. Is someone watching me, wondering, perhaps, why that strange girl has just walked over the bridge and back?

At the bottom I hesitate. In the end, I take the road down by Octopus and on to Mill Road. I stop at a baker's and buy two cakes. I eat them hungrily, shoving them into my mouth. Passers-by avert their eyes. The rain has stopped and the sun is glinting off the muddy puddles at the side of the road.

When I get home, my mother is there. She has taken that afternoon off work. She asks me what library book I got out. I say I couldn't find one I liked. I can sense her disapproval.

Dinner is a stony affair. Martha has gone to a gig.

Friday comes and goes. I eat. My nails look horrible.

I sleep most of Saturday and get up at two. The house is silent. I go downstairs and get the crumpets out of the freezer. I toast them, one by one, and butter them. The butter melts and congeals on the plate. At the end I scrape it off and eat it.

I hear the door open. My mother has been shopping with Martha. They come into the kitchen, my mother with a Sainsbury's bag, Martha with a large Gap bag. She shows me her new sweatshirt. My mother looks at the crumpets.

"All of them?" she asks.

I look at my feet. I feel like a nine year old caught with her hand in the sweetie jar.

"I was hungry," I reply sorrowfully.

She bangs her packages down and clears up, rolling her eyes. Martha sulks. I have spoiled the happy mood of their shopping trip. My mother puts crumpets on the shopping list. She is in a bad mood until dinner, when my father comes home. They want to take us to Welney tomorrow to watch the swans. Martha grumbles. I eat. My mother smiles brightly. We are going to enjoy tomorrow she says. She is trying too hard.

*

I get up early on Sunday. The house is completely silent, save for the ticking of the clocks. The clock in my room has stopped. Outside the hours and minutes pass, but in my room it is always five thirty-nine.

Boredom is slowly turning to depression. My grandmother rings up. We talk, until Martha runs in and snatches the telephone, to tell her about the Junction. I watch *Between the Lines* on video again. Martha joins me halfway through. She "really fancies" Neil Pearson. He's "well horny". I can't see it.

After lunch we all put on jeans and heavy sweaters, and my father gets our wellies out of the shed. I feel fat. My mother, watching us both, is no doubt wondering how Martha can manage to look glamorous in wellies and an Arran, whereas I still look fat and ugly in my best clothes. She does not say this, just observes that I need a hair cut.

Amira Mitchell (14)

There is a flood on the road on the way to Welney, so we have to take another route round. It takes us an hour to get there. It is around four when we do arrive. My German teacher is just leaving. She and my mother have a jolly conversation in the car-park.

We have to cross a wooden bridge to get to the hide. I can see the water, lying still, unmoving, beneath the wooden slats. The hide is very quiet. My parents fuss around with the binoculars. Martha gets out her magazine.

As it darkens, the swans and ducks return to roost. My parents keep pointing at the sky and trying to make me and Martha watch the birds flying in. I am not interested. For the past hour I have been watching one bird, a little brown duck, swimming around. Unlike the other birds, it has no obvious partners. It keeps approaching other, larger birds, but they rebuff it with vicious pecks.

At five thirty Martha starts to whine. It's cold, and she's missing the charts. We leave.

When we get home my mother hugs me. It was fun, after all, she reminds me. I don't like to disillusion her. She does love me, she tells me unconvincingly, when I don't answer. I frown. Martha is a more deserving recipient of her maternal fondness.

Later that evening, my parents have an argument with Martha. I listen with half an ear.

On Monday everything is back to normal. Martha is still in a mood, and leaves early. My mother has to go to the dentist and my father has a meeting. The days stretch ahead of me, long and unending. I will probably spend them all in the same way, television and eating.

I finish all the Easter eggs for breakfast, then make myself a plate of toast and a tomato. I take all the blue willow pattern plates out of the cupboard and lay them on the table.

I choose the least chipped, the one with the most pleasing shade of blue. Never having possessed it myself, beauty is important to me. At three I decide to do something. I go into town. In Sainsbury's, buying a chocolate mousse, I overhear two sisters arguing.

A: I can make really BIG pops with Silly Putty.

B: So can I . . . I've been practising.

A: [Scornfully] I don't need to practise.

I leave, and go on to Christ's Pieces to eat my purchase. I have no spoon, and so have to use my fingers. I can see the pity on the faces of the shoppers. Sometimes I pity myself.

I am late home. When I enter, my mother and sister are sitting at the kitchen table, chatting. They look up as I enter and offer me a piece of the cake that Martha has made. I accept, and go up the stairs cramming it into my mouth.

After dinner my father comes up to my room. He sits awkwardly on my chair and smiles. He has found his old turntable, he says. Do I want it? I nod grudgingly. I have wanted a record player for a long time, but this is in the nature of a peace settlement. Building bridges.

Tuesday. I lock myself into the bathroom and weigh myself for the first time in weeks. The needle hovers uncertainly around sixty kilograms. I cannot believe it. I have gained nearly six kilograms. Pulling on a shirt and leggings, I sit down at my desk to plan a diet. I have not eaten anything today and that is how it's going to stay. No breakfast, I decide emphatically, no lunch and certainly no snacks.

It can't be too hard, I reason. Martha is always dieting. I go into my mother's room and pull out the family photo album from the wardrobe. In the front, after the pictures of Martha, are photos of me as a child. I am rather pleased with the little girl in the pictures. She has pretty blonde hair and a rather sweet smile. She stares into the camera with confidence, but not arrogance. I wonder what has happened to the little girl; where she has gone.

I go into town, this time to the library. I have to choose a topic for the talk that everyone in my class has to do for GCSE Oral English. I want to do a famous person – it'll be easy, all I have to do is get a biography out. So I head over to the biographies.

I start by choosing a letter at random, and scan all the "I"s, then the "J"s. I am about to settle for Edith Jones, a missionary in Chile 1914–57, when I see a title that looks interesting. *Buried Alive*, by Myra Friedman. The writer has the same name as me. I pull it out and read the introduction. It is a biography of Janis Joplin. I have heard my parents mention her – there was a film made about her as well. I shrug, and take both the books to get them out.

On the way home I overhear two girls sitting on a park bench. One, pinching her calf, says regretfully, "I think I'm too thin. I'd like a bit more fat on my legs."

Too thin? How can anyone be too thin?

Back home I head for the fridge but stop myself in time. I do not feel very hungry, it is the temptation, the overwhelming need to eat. I do not know if I can work without eating. I take my books upstairs and read the introductions to both of them. Edith Jones sounds incredibly boring. I settle down to read the Janis Joplin.

It is nearly six o'clock when I finish. My mother has come home and is moving around downstairs. I don't think that she realizes I am in. I do not move for a while after closing the book. All sorts of thoughts are jumbled together in my head. I feel like somebody has touched me deep inside.

At dinner my father asks me what I plan to write my talk about. I tell him. Martha and my mother exchange glances. I frown, trying to keep back tears. They can never support me in anything I do. Their amusement is almost palpable.

"Wasn't Janis Joplin the really ugly one who topped herself?" asked Martha.

I rise to the bait. Slamming my chair back against the wall, I leave the table. I am ravenously hungry, but at least it will help me to diet. As I go up the stairs I hear my mother say censoriously, "Martha".

I have begun to feel incredibly protective towards the memory of Janis. I think of her now as Janis. I expect hundreds of depressed teenagers have taken her up as a heroine at some time.

Martha avoids me before she leaves. Wednesday. I have survived a whole week. One down, one to go. I go into town and watch the people. I sort them in my mind: thin, medium, fat. I am definitely the latter.

When I get home I go through my shelves and pull out a notebook. I have hundreds, hidden after numerous failed attempts to keep diaries. Concentrating hard, I write a list of foods I cannot eat. No margarine on my bread, no salt on my food. Only water to drink. I have not eaten anything yet today. My stomach rumbles and I feel slightly faint and shaky, but my resolve is unshaken. I put some music on the cassette player and roll on to my back. I grit my teeth. I have always hated exercise, but it is the lesser of two evils. I do bicycles for three minutes and leg lifts for another two. Afterwards I lie sprawled on the floor. My legs are killing me, but I feel that pain with pleasure. The first step to a new me.

My mother comes home and offers me a slice of chocolate cake. I refuse virtuously.

For dinner I have a small portion of spaghetti bolognese. I shake my head to salt and scrape the majority of the meat off. When I explain that I am on a diet my mother smiles, gratified. Martha smiles knowingly. My father concentrates on his food. I sit, silent and hungry as they eat their dessert. I think about food. A big plate of fish and chips, chocolate fudge cake, fudge sundae . . . My reverie is interrupted by the end of the meal. Later that night I wander into the kitchen. There is a bowl of peanuts on the side. I scoop up a handful and put them into my mouth. I have chewed and swallowed them before I realize what I am doing. I feel immediately sick. Salted peanuts. We were told in school once, how much fat salted peanuts contain. I cannot remember. A lot. I spit out what I still have in my mouth and rinse out the sink. I wash my mouth out several times and then go upstairs. I do one hundred leg lifts each side.

The next day is warmer. I get up late, and want breakfast. There is nothing to do: I usually avert boredom by eating. I want to weigh myself, but daren't in case I haven't lost enough weight. I do all the workouts on daytime television.

Louise rings up. She wants me to go into town, but I tell her that I'm going away and I have to pack. I don't want anyone to see me as I am. They can't see me until I am free, purged of fat. I want to be so thin that people will remark on it. I want to be exceptional.

I listen to the news. At the end is a special item, about Jim Morrison. He would have been fifty today. I have a terrible feeling. I pick up *Buried Alive* and flick into two or three pages. And there it is in black and white, "born on 19 January 1943". She would have been fifty last year. Anger swells up inside me. They didn't celebrate for her. I begin to cry. The birthday they forgot.

I go downstairs and into the larder. I pull open the pack of doughnuts and eat them, all six, greedily. I lick the sugar out of the plastic. I must look like an animal. I open the golden syrup and pour it into my mouth. It runs out the side and down on my neck and shirt. The cooking chocolate. I

Laura Carlton (14)

rip it open and eat it: four, five, even six squares at a time. Cheerios, jam, chocolate spread, tortilla chips, sun-dried tomatoes, olive oil, brown sugar, salad cream, tomato ketchup, pasta sauce, perfect and juicy in its squat little jar.

Fridge. Nothing much here. Maple sugar and cheese.

I pull open the freezer. I am concentrating now, engaged in my own private marathon. All the Kit-Kats in their shiny paper, frozen naan bread, ice cream . . . I need a spoon for it. I take the box into the kitchen and pause. The syrup is sticky on my throat. I touch my fingers to it and lick it off. Like blood from an open wound. My mouth, my stomach, they are my wounds.

My stomach jerks and I think I am going to be sick. But

I am not. Then suddenly I realize what I have done. Sugar, fat. I disgust myself. All the calories I have just poured into myself. Greedy bitch. I am swelling up, I can feel it now. Fatter and fatter. I have to do something, but what? I can't be sick, never have been able to. Besides, that would be a cop out, wouldn't it? I have to punish myself for what I've done. I've given in.

open the drawers nothing suitable in there   over on the side in the container   the bread knife   not sharp enough   the vegetable knife sharp yes sharp enough   the serrated edges are glinting   I bring it down on my forearm and slash   oh god it hurts god it hurts   don't stop punish yourself you bitch   more up the arms now and something is running over my hand and on to the floor   and I can't see what it is

the whole of my left arm is crimson   god it hurts

Alex McRae (14)

*As Parents Fight

Squinting at the yellow sun
Which asks no questions
The child shrinks away from the circus.

Flying balls and spinning plates
The lions roar as they eat their tamer
She screams in her apron.
But the clown's face twists like Plasticine
And his eyes are burning
The flame thrower belches fiery spurts
And the circus dog yelps and scrabbles
To avoid his crushing boots.

In the corner, the smallest juggler crouches
Squinting through her tears.

Rachel Simmonds (14)

Emma Richmond (14)

My Canine Dad

My Daddy (strange as it might seem)
Is very like Cora my dog.

My Dad has a very small, soft, secretive smile,
But you can always tell when he has it.
Of course dogs cannot smile,
But Cora can.
Maybe I'm imagining it,
But sometimes I can see a smile
Just a small one,
Identical to Dad's.
Their bright eyes give it away.

They both work on the farm each day.
No change, whatever the weather may bring.
"They are both allowed in at night," says Mum,
"But only if they are clean."

Then Cora curls up in front of the stove,
Staying warm, safe in our kitchen,
While Dad sits comfy in his armchair.
Their faces both show contentment for now,
As they share that same blank expression.
Nobody will ever really know
What Cora and Dad are thinking.
This is what I find most similar and lovable about these two,
That they are both so mysterious.

Now, I'm not saying that Cora is half man,
Or that Daddy is half dog.
I'm saying only that my Cora is Cora,
and that my Daddy is Dad.

Anna Woollen (8)

My Rabbit

My rabbit loves
to eat her greens
and bites us
when she's
feeling mean
Daddy calls her
Sid Vicious
and also thinks
she'd be
delicious

Tim Scrace (16)

David Newman (9)

Even if I Could Rely on Dad, Could I Trust the Christmas Post?

Sometimes I wish my Mam would do things *before* I got home from school. Things like go to the post office and stand in great queues. Great, long queues are dead boring, but she said we had to go to post the Christmas presents so that we didn't have to go driving out to deliver them when the car had problems. Mam's car always has problems. Not just this car. All of them. I don't mean she has lots of them because she hasn't, but every time she has one there's something wrong with it just when we need it to work properly. And the post office was really crowded.

Everybody was posting parcels and I started to think that maybe everybody in Ashington had broken down cars and then just when it was our turn and Mam started putting our parcels on the scales I had this fantastic idea. I waited till she'd finished then I leaned on the scales. It said £5.50 First Class and £3.28 Second Class. Mmm, I thought . . . this is a good idea. Maybe I could get me posted to Dad's. That way I could play on his computer as often as I wanted and it would save Mam having to get people to push the car and it would save petrol. In fact she needn't even leave the house, I could do it all myself. In fact maybe it would be best if I didn't tell her. She'd probably say it was a bad idea. Grown-ups aren't very good at knowing what good ideas are. They usually think boring things are good ideas. Like standing in queues and posting parcels instead of going out in the car and breaking down and having some fun being pushed and towed and things. Mmm. I'd best go first class I decided. And I would need a big box to go in. That would be easy though because we always have boxes from the food we buy because my Mam won't buy plastic bags. She says why should we buy bags when we've already bought the food. So if the bags aren't free, we get a box and usually we get boxes. My Grandma collects them. She has big ones and little ones and likes us to give her them back when we've used them. Actually she lets the rabbit have them to play with because she likes him. She likes us as well sometimes. So we get to borrow them. Grandad has to get them. And she gets cross if he brings the wrong size. She likes them to have strong sides and lids and firm bottoms and that's just what I would need for my journey.

You see, we go to Dad's usually on a Saturday and sometimes on a Friday but at the moment Mam's car keeps breaking down. Usually it gets there but it takes ages and ages and it shakes and shudders and I keep bumping my head. Mam's got the steering wheel to hold on to but I haven't and we sort of jump along the road. People stare at us and sometimes they have to push.

It would be OK if Dad had a car but he hasn't. Dianne has one but he isn't allowed to use it because he hasn't passed his test. Actually me and Mam have seen him drive it. He reversed it one day to put it in its own place outside their door and it took him ages. We clapped him when he had finished. Mam says it's time he took a test because he can drive. She taught him when I was little but one day he was going so fast that when he stopped he didn't brake fast enough and we nearly went right over the edge of the road at St Cuthbert's Village and there was about a twenty-foot drop. It was a Lada and Dad said it was like *The Italian Job* which is a film where a bus nearly goes over a cliff. Anyway he doesn't drive now.

And what with Mam's car needing pushing all the time it means I don't get to play on Dad's computer as much as I want. That means he gets more practice than me and probably he'll be able to beat me. Actually I doubt that but I'd like to go there more often.

I don't really mind Mam's car. Grandma does though. You should hear her complain about it. She makes Mam stop and let her get out then she wipes the windscreen with her hanky. Mam says she hopes it's a clean one because we don't want snots all over the windscreen. We've got enough problems. My Grandma says being in our car is like riding a kangaroo. I don't know how she knows that though because I don't think my Grandma has never been on a kangaroo. She would probably say she had though if I asked her because grown-ups say stupid things like that sometimes. It's best to pretend you believe them.

So anyway I had to plan how to get to Dad's house. I'd never had such a good idea and it might not even cost money. Well not my money anyway. You see sometimes the stamps can be paid after the parcel is delivered. I know that because I got a parcel from Michael Jackson in Los Angeles and the postman knocked on the door with it. It was dead early on a Saturday morning and we were all asleep. My stepdad Pete had to pay the postman twelve pounds eighty so we could have the parcel and we all went to the door. He's not really my stepdad but he's sort of. It's complicated. Actually Peter asked who the parcel was for and he went back to bed when it wasn't for him. So did I in case I had to pay the postman out of my money. Joe didn't though he stayed there maybe hoping that the postman would give him the parcel. Peter and Joe are my sort of stepbrothers like Pete is my stepdad. Like I said it's all a bit complicated in our house. Mam says sometimes families are. She was in her dressing-grown and she rang the post office to complain but in the end Pete paid the money and we got the parcel. So that meant I could post me without the stamps on.

Then I remembered. Dad liked a lie-in on Saturdays. What if he didn't answer the door when the postman knocked? I could maybe end up being stuck in a box all the weekend and nobody would know where I was. I couldn't tell Dad I was coming because he might not think it was a good idea and anyway I wanted it to be a surprise for him. Then there was just one other thing. What if Dad didn't have the money to pay the postman? Sometimes Dad said he had no money. I never usually believed him but what if it was true and he couldn't afford to pay for me being delivered? There was Dianne who could pay. Dad is married to Dianne now and that's complicated too. Like when we did the Swimathon, me and Mam and Dad and Dianne, people asked if Dianne was my sister and we had to say she was Dad's wife and they looked ever so confused.

Yes. She would pay the postman. Then I thought that maybe she might have gone out. Sometimes when me and Mam got to Dad's Dianne had already gone out early because she was good at getting up Dad said. It was then I got to thinking that maybe this wasn't such a bright idea after all. Well it was a good idea. But what if I couldn't rely on the grown-ups? Sometimes they're not very reliable.

That night I thought about it in bed. I like to think in private and bed is the most private place in our house. Actually there's the bathroom but the problem is I like lying down to think and that would mean having to lie on the floor where it would be cold or get in the bath and it wasn't a Sunday. Baths on a Sunday were bad enough. Anyway, Mam might get suspicious if I got in the bath on a Thursday. So I lay in bed to think and put the television on. It was *Northern Life* and at first I ignored it because sometimes news is so boring and then there was a post office and lots of people and they were talking about dates and how you have to post things early at Christmas and how the post takes longer. It was then I started to listen to what they were saying. They were talking to people about the post and they were complaining about how long presents were taking to get to places. I remembered that my stepbrother Peter had waited ages for a parcel that he'd ordered and my Mam had said about having to post the things before it got too near the time. Mind Peter's parcel had the wrong postcode on. It said "ME" instead of "NE" so we think it maybe went all the way round Merseyside before we got it. So if I posted me I'd have to be sure I got the postcode right. Unless I wanted to travel around I suppose . . .

I thought about my plan. And it was a good plan I knew that. It was a very good plan but maybe . . . well just maybe . . . What with Dad and his lie-ins and maybe him not having money . . . and the fact that it was near Christmas . . . maybe I should forget it for now. Like I said it was a fantastic idea. One of the best ones I had ever had but because of Dad . . . and the other grown-ups maybe I should leave it for now. It was a very good plan. Fantastic even. But well . . . I suppose, even if I could rely on Dad . . . Could I trust the Christmas Post?

Nazmin Khan (10)

*Hiding Place

Some evenings, me and my cousins,
Rahat, Sabrina and Prianca,
tip-toe upstairs to the airing cupboard.
Inside, the boiler is covered in plastic.
I call it a nappy. Prianca says
it's a baby boiler.
It's sweltering in there,
but we don't care.
We turn it into the Spy Club.
While we talk, we eat chocolate chip
cookies and drink mugs of hot chocolate.
We send Rahat to creep downstairs
to see what's happening,
and wait in the dark for his message.

Edel McArdle (10)

A Jolly Uncle

One day, Robert's uncle came to tea. He was a very large and jolly uncle. He sat Robert on his knee, and bounced him up and down. Robert didn't like it very much – but his uncle seemed to like bouncing him, so he sat as politely as he could. Then, "Thank you very much," he said, "but I would like to stop now."

He tumbled down from his uncle's knee and crept under the table, where Graham was sitting with his woolly hat pulled down over his eyes. "Has he gone?" asked Graham. "No," said Robert. As he spoke, the corner of the tablecloth was lifted, and the big, smiling face of his uncle appeared. "Well, well, well!" he said. "What's all this?" He held out his empty hand, felt behind Robert's ear, and brought out a shining five pence piece. Robert was very pleased. "Shall I do it again?" asked his uncle. "Yes, please!" said Robert, and he scrambled from beneath the table, and stood by his uncle's knee. Robert's uncle felt behind Robert's right ear and brought out another five penny piece. "Thank you," said Robert, and he went back under the table to show Graham.

But Graham just sniffed, and pulled his hat further down over his eyes. "What's the matter?" said Robert. "Nothing," said Graham. But something was the matter, he looked greener and smaller – so small that he seemed to be disappearing beneath his hat.

"Please don't go!" said Robert – for he knew that Graham could do anything he wished. He could make himself as big as a house or he could vanish altogether.

"Don't go," he said again but Graham just became smaller and smaller. "You don't want me anymore now that you've got your magical uncle." He made himself so small that he couldn't be seen. "Please come back!" said Robert. "It isn't magic. It's a trick."

"A trick?" said Graham coming back at once and putting his hat back on. "Are you sure?" "Of course," said Robert, and he took one of the five penny pieces and held it between his fingers. He held it by the edge, so that Graham could see the coin sticking out at the back. Graham took the coin, and held it in his paw, just as Robert had done. Then, very gently, he felt behind Robert's ear, and brought the coin out. He was very pleased with himself and he did the trick six times before he gave the money back to Robert. Then he took Robert on his knee, and bounced him up and down, as Robert's uncle had done.

"Thank you," said Robert. "Thank you very much, thank you very much indeed."

Then he lay on his back and laughed – for he knew that even though his uncle was peering under the table, he couldn't see how Graham was sitting and bringing pennies from behind his ears, hundreds of pennies, thousands of pennies, hundreds and thousands of pennies, hundreds and thousands and millions of pennies.

TIME CAPSULES

Caroline Murray-Lyon (11)

Louise Bevan (9)

Listen

I can hear a pearl
slip off mum's ear-ring.
I can hear mould
grow on apples;
the juice drip to the ground.
I can hear my teacher
thinking of what to do next.
I can hear ladybird's wings.
I can hear glue sticking into place.
I can hear the Vikings
splashing towards the shore.
I can hear the words in my poem
re-order themselves on the page.

Lucy Jack (13)

*Memories

A Victorian Scrap-book

"For darling Sally", it says inside.
In 1895 this book was started,
In 1942 it closed.

Crumpled brown pages,
Depicting years of work;
Sticking and pasting,
Cutting, collecting.

Its old, green, leathery cover
Sheltering hundreds of tiny cards,
Miniature floral scraps.

"With blessings rich and fair,
The New Year come to thee!"
It says, the crumpled satin card
Foxed at the edges.

A great-grandmother,
Writing for a baby
Who will remember nothing
But the scrap-book and her Nana's name.

Timothy Wilson (9)

Dreams

I rush on the expanse of ice,
Zooming past the odd slow person.
Then I come to the end of the rink.
The end of my dreams,
For I cannot skate.

Speeding on the snow,
Skis swerving round the red flags.
Now the slalom's over, I can relax
In a very comfy,
Soft armchair.

But that was dreams,
Now I'm on proper snow,
And I don't know
What to do!

William Gold (13)

Guy Burton (12)

James Forbes Robertson (11)

James Hall (11)

Zoë Brigley (13)

*The Box

Pull back the silken, silver scarf,
Take out the glowing box,
Covered in silver shells like moonbeams,
And try its golden key.

Out comes the sophisticated cat
With bright, green eyes,
Who hisses and claws
At the common dogs.

Out comes the protester,
Shouting with banners
To save the whale
And stop killing elephants.

Next comes fear holding a dentist's drill,
With an evil glint in his eyes.
Then the aspirations of the Jungfrau Joch Mountains
Touching the clouds above,
Beautiful but so cold
Under that texture of pure ice.

Out walks an old lady limping badly,
Who falls down
To a black, shadowy pool
Into a skeleton's arms.

Nazmin Khan (10)

*Prianca

When I change her nappy,
I tickle her tummy
with my nose, and
she tugs my hair.
Her teeth are like
grains of rice.
I feel her soggy thumb.
When she says, "So",
she sounds like Donald Duck.

Elizabeth Holden (8)

*The Croft

A cold winter's night.
Blankets wrapped round the toddlers.
Babies asleep in their cribs,
swaying in their dreams.
Wind rapping on the thin window panes.

She throws a match into the fire.
Wild horse flames prance
in the moonlight.

Oliver Densham (12)

*Glass Jars

I opened the door,
And saw . . .
A shelf of posts,
Posts of light,
Lazers,
Holding up screw-top halos . . .
I switched on the light.
Jars.
I walked over, inspected the shelf.

Dulcie Titchiner (12)

Martin Bonger (10)

A jar of fire,
Round and flickering.
An exaggerated grate
Which ballooned up from the hearth.
A cat,
Ghostly,
Moved through the jars,
Tried to find an empty space,
Finally settled . . .
And I moved on.
A window,
Purposeless in a room of glass.
A bare light,
Hung from the screw-on ceiling
Of a strange, cylindrical world.
No visible electric source.
Again,
Another jar, containing a sink,
Curved and distorted,
An enamelled banana,

Piled high with dishes
In the dirty, curling water.
And finally me.
Only me.
Giant body and tiny head,
A human bottle,
With distorted features in the curving glass.
But I was free,
Not imprisoned
In a jar,
Preserved under a waxed-paper sky.
I went, leaving the world on the shelf,
And turned off the light,
Leaving the halos,
Supported on sticks.
Angel lamp-posts,
One-legged coffee tables.

Sylvan Friend (11)

*Holding Chickens

I used to hold chickens.
They felt plump like a pot-bellied pig.
Their bodies were warm like a hot-water bottle.
Their feet were scritchy-scratchy as they tried to grip.
They tried to flap their fluffy wings.
They felt as though they were just about
To enlarge and explode.
Sometimes I didn't hold them properly
And they got their slippery feathers free
And flapped them in my face.
They started making squawking noises
And went mad and jumped
Out of my hands and hopped and ran around.
Then all the other chickens went mad
And I got fed up with them
And left them to squabble among themselves.

Evan Brown (13)

*The Old Pavilion

By the edge of the deserted playing field,
Under the white-capped mountain,
Thrown up into the sky by a force which is dormant now,
There is a tin-roofed shack, barely standing,
Timbers warped and rotting.

They play here sometimes,
And the field hosts a game of football,
A gang of kids with a ball, one evening,
Wishing it were Ibrox or Wembley,
But not here, under the white-capped mountain,
No, not here!

And the concrete porch acts as the stand,
Where substitutes wait,
Swerving on bikes until they are chosen.
Sometimes, those who brave the bitter morning cold,
Are fans who shout and cheer,
Leaning against the old walls,
Gazing through the holes where the wood has given way,
But a padlock still secures the hingeless door.

Through the window, a light-fitting dangles,
Rocking to and fro in the draught that whines in the shadows,
While forgotten equipment lies mouldering,
Time-capsules from days that are long since gone.

For once, long before these children of today,
Long before the moles pushed tunnels through the green,
Other children would have thronged about this place,
Changing to compete out on the field, or playing on the concrete terraces,
Games we have now forgotten.

Faded graffiti scratched on the weather-beaten walls testify to times
Before the iron lock was rusted to the door-frame,
When the wood was new and strong,
And people knew its purpose well.
But the children who carved there then,
Have gone.

Scott Killick (8)

*Fun with the Soldiers

One morning me and my brother Michael were feeling bored so we decided to play at being soldiers. My mum was clearing the breakfast dishes away so me and my brother Michael sneaked into the living-room and put some soot on our faces from the chimney of our coal fire – it was safe because it was not lit. We told my mum that we would be on the forestry drive if she needed us. We walked towards the drive and we saw a jeep. It looked like an army one so we walked a little bit closer and saw that there were two jeeps and one truck. Me and my brother planned to spy on them, we both had our walkie-talkies on us. Michael managed to get across the drive and we followed the army men up the drive hiding behind them. When the army men turned around, me and my brother kept talking to each other on our walkie-talkies. You see, they were the baddies and we were the goodies. We got to the top of the drive and we saw that there were more army men with some electrical equipment. Just then I heard my brother say come in come in on the walkie-talkie. My brother told me that the baddies were sending messages to the head boss so there might be more baddies coming so we must cause a distraction. I asked what is that, Michael said don't worry leave it to me so I sat and waited. The army men seemed to get mad with the equipment and one of the army men went back down the forestry drive. The others were still shouting then I heard a crackle in the trees across the drive. The army men went quiet and walked to where the noise came from holding their guns in their hands. I sneaked up to the equipment. I got quite close to it when my brother shouted over the walkie-talkie, run Scott, get help, they've got me. I was scared and started to run. I looked behind me while I was running to see if they were coming and BANG, I hit a tree. I lay there for a moment and when I opened my eyes the army men were around me, two of them had their guns pointed at me and one of them said you are our prisnor my brother told them we were only playing prettend soldiers. I was scared now, some of the army men were laughing at us and one asked us what we had got on our faces, I told them it was soot and they laughed again.

The army man I saw earlyer going down the forestry drive was walking towards us and he started talking to the one in charge, and they looked at us, and asked if we lived in the cottage below the forestry drive and we said yes. We were surprised when they said well why didn't you tell us that you have a nice mum. She even let us use the telephone to phone head quarters to tell them our equipment is not working, and then the army man asked us if we had seen army guns before and we said no so they showed us how to use them. We had a good time with the guns. Then they let us drive in their truck, it was brilliant and me and my brother had a fun day and the army men were only kidding when they said we were their prisoners.

The end – this is a true story.

Amanda George (15)

**Something Gets to Them

"Are you ever coming?" asked the boy.

"Soon," she said. She knew he would not go fishing without her. He had bought bait, made sandwiches, filled a bottle with lemonade, sorted his tackle – everything was put ready by the open door. He was waiting outside the door in the sunlight.

"Come on it's late."

"It's not."

"What are you doing?"

She was at the mirror by the sink fixing her hair into a pony-tail with a new tortoiseshell clip. Trying to.

"I'll go alone."

She just knew he wouldn't. It was for her to watch him bait up, watch him cast; to wait patiently, clamping her lips together not to make a noise; to defer to his patience, knowledge and skill; to fix her eyes upon the striving line. He wanted someone to wail his disappointment if he lost a fish, to leap and shout his satisfaction if one swung clear of the water and fell twitching silver upon the green at their feet. And he preferred that she should be the one to relate to his father in the evening, sipping his mother's lovely sweet cocoa by the fire – "I watched Robert catch two trout."

Or three, or four, or five, once I caught a fish alive. She sang the rhyme as they walked along. She'd had to leave her hair loose. It was like a black mane, too thick and wiry for the new clip. She was used to it round her shoulders but it made her hotter. Today it was sweating hot and there were a lot of flies – the high strong sun, no wind, no clouds.

"Robert let's stop here."

"We're going to the loop," said Robert. His father's farm had water meadows, but Robert had planned that they should cross by the road bridge and fish away from home on the opposite bank on Ron Evans' land. The fishing was better, in fact Ron had let it to a London doctor: "You'll be all right. He only comes down weekends," Ron had said. A public footpath ran along his bank, skirting two meadows before the river curled back on itself in a wide, deep loop. Ron's Herefords were grazing in the second meadow.

They reached the place where Ron's meadow bordered the inner curl of the loop. The high bank here jutted out almost like an island: to the right and left of it willow trees stuck out their branches over the shining mirror beneath them. This island made a fine curving stretch of water, deep under this bank and in mid-stream levelling out to stony shallows by the farther bank, where trees drooped in suspense above the still water. These shallow pools under the willows were great places for resting trout, likewise the deep water under the overhang on which they were standing. The almost imperceptible current, unfortified by any breath of wind, hung merely a transparent veil between the rocks and roots of the river bed proper and the shafts of sunlight which cleaved clear to the bottom. In this clarity the children's sharp eyes missed nothing.

"By Christ, there's a big 'un!" She also had seen a large fish lying along the current in mid-stream. Quickly and excitedly Robert dumped the gear. He began to fix up his rod.

"Get us a worm out."

She found a piece of flat slate from a place where the bank fell away, and went for the bait tin. She so hated the warm feel of the tin and the stirring of the white grubs within which made her stomach heave. She shut her eyes and held her nose with her free hand, offering him the tin at arm's length.

"Yuk!" she said "Ugh, horrible!"

Robert knew, but he didn't care. He picked at a worm, fixed it to the hook, reeled out sufficient line.

"Keep still."

"I'm putting the tin back."

"He can see us easy. It's too bright."

He cast quite skilfully up-river from the resting trout, they watched the white blob of worm wriggling its way down the current. Robert reeled in gently, bringing the bait within striking distance. The fish ignored it as it floated past.

"Try again," said Robert. He tried a dozen times. She sat on the dry grass, relaxed, quietly absorbing the rhythm of his movements. Today she felt withdrawn and careless of his success or failure. She was thinking. "I'm never going to open the bait tin again." And she was thinking, "That fish lives there, it's his home," when suddenly the fish was there no longer.

Robert looked up. "Bloody cows," he said. Upstream from them the Herefords were ambling into the water at a shallow muddy place, some stopping to drink, others stood cooling their heels.

"Stupid bloody animals. Go and chase them off," Robert said.

"You go," she said. She held his rod while he ran along the bank shouting and waving at the cows. While he was gone she saw a small fish jump. Also she saw the incredible lightning-blue flash of a kingfisher. He skimmed the water's surface in front of her, travelling the surprising curve of the loop with brilliant precision. She thought, he must know all of the winding shapes of the river. Before he got to the loop he must have remembered the shape of it, to go so fast.

Robert came back, hot.

"I saw a kingfisher," she said.

"I wish Ron didn't turn his cows into that meadow." He

took the rod from her. They both saw a fish jump, near the other bank.

"Only a little one. There's not enough wind, the big 'uns are all lying close. There'll be a few lying under this bank." He dropped the worm straight down in front of where they both crouched. Quite soon, a smallish fish ventured out from beneath their feet, Robert swayed the rod top, the worm danced obediently to his baton, weaving a tiny pattern in the water.

"Come on, come on!" He moved the rod a little more. The worm responded and the fish darted away.

"You ought to hold it still."

"I know what I'm doing. They're used to things moving. They're all fed already – they've had plenty."

"There's not many mayfly."

"That's why they're not jumping."

"They don't jump for mayfly, they wait till they get waterlogged."

"What do they jump for then?"

"They jump for joy."

"Oh don't talk daft!"

"They do. I read it."

"They jump for bloody mayfly. Everyone knows that." She pointed. A sizeable trout had leaped some distance downstream, the rings lapped gently wider.

"I'll try there." She made no move to follow him.

"I'm going to have a drink." The lemonade Robert had mixed was weak and tepid, but she was thirsty. And hungry. She opened the sandwiches. Brown bread with honey in. She counted them, he had made four double slices and cut them in half.

"Four halves each." She called to him.

"It's not teatime."

"I'm hungry."

"Shut up shouting."

She lay on her stomach on the warm green, munching sandwiches and staring into the water. The big trout they had first seen was back again. She tried to imagine herself looking out from his angle at the sun, at the willows and at her own self looking down. She reckoned he was big enough to defend the place that was his home against all other fish, and at night it would be a safe place. No poachers along the bank could reach him there. Fish were wily and wary, but fishermen were crafty and skilful. She hoped that the big trout could feel the altered flow of the current at his back when a strong nylon fishing line sliced the water in two; that he could see the line like a thin crack in his watery window as he stared through it up at the sunlight. She hoped he knew the danger of it.

Robert was making his way back. He looked tall, striding along. His jeans were tucked into his wellingtons, and his checked shirt was tucked into his jeans at the front – it was out at the back. Before he reached her she picked up a stone and threw it into the water.

"What are you doing? What are you chucking stones for?" He sounded peevish. She glanced at where the big fish had been.

"You should know not to chuck stones."

"Have a sandwich." She held the packet out. He took one and ate it absent-mindedly, staring into the water.

"They are just not interested. Not a single bite. It's no good today."

She knew his mood: blaming the sunshine, the lack of wind, blaming the mayfly, blaming her for speaking, moving.

"D'you want to go home?" she asked.

"We only just got here."

"If you didn't want to fish we could bathe. It's hot."

"It's too bloody bright, we need a bit of wind. If you hadn't have shouted at me up there – I nearly had a bite."

"It's no fun if you can't talk."

"You'd better bloody go home then."

A bathe, she thought. A lovely cool bathe.

"Hey look," said Robert, "There's that big 'un again."

"He's too wily; you'll never catch him."

"Want to bet?"

She clenched her fists and stared at the line where it entered the water, willing the fish to sense danger. She did not watch the bait as it drew nearer to the fish, she watched the motionless fish himself, willing him to stay still, to ignore it, not to feel hungry, not to feel tempted: no, no, no. Robert kept drawing the worm across. She counted. She had breathed "no" under her breath. Robert had tried ten times; ten skilful, careful attempts, and each time, no.

"You've tried ten times. He doesn't want to know."

Robert cast again. Get past thirteen, let him get past thirteen. She picked up a small stone. Tense and nervous, she held it. She held her breath.

"Fourteen," she said, fingering the stone.

"Quit counting. You've got to have patience, you've got to spend hours. Quit that stupid counting."

But still she counted. Twenty casts. Then the hook caught itself in a piece of weed and the worm came off.

"Get the bait tin".

"You get it," she said. She jumped up and walked away a little.

"You're no help. What d'you come out for I wonder?" Robert was cross. He put his rod down and went for the tin. While his back was turned she quickly threw the little stone. Robert heard the splash, turned and saw the rings in the water and saw that the fish was gone.

"He's gone! You threw another stone!"

"No I didn't!"

"You bloody did. I heard it."

"Something fell into the water."

"Oh yes, bloody likely, out of the sky, right by my fish, scared him off—"

"It must have."

"You try to fool me—"

I don't like Robert.

"You chuck stones—"

I don't like him.

" – and then tell lies you didn't."

I hate him.

"I hate you," she said.

"Well, I hate people who tell lies. You're no fisherman."

"No I'm not. I hate fishing. I'm glad I scared him off."

"Well, hard luck," said Robert, "because he's back. If you're stopping, keep your hands in your bloody pockets."

Miserable, she now hated the fish. She didn't care what happened to him. He deserves to be caught – good riddance to him; another stupid fish could have his place. All she had done for him, and there he was, stupid, back in the same place, mesmerized by the stupid horrible worm. Persistently Robert repeated the same routine. She lost count – hundreds of times – for ever.

"Oh, so boring!" she said loudly. "I think fishing is so stupid!" But she failed to goad him because just then the fish moved slightly. Robert was holding the worm steady about four inches from his nose and he altered his position fractionally.

"Come on, come on," muttered Robert, "come on, come on—"

"He won't," she said, again loudly.

"Shut up!" Robert's voice was muted and savage. The fish

moved again, but still maintaining the same distance between him and the bait.

"He will. Come on." Robert moved the worm half an inch closer. Nothing.

Suddenly a much smaller fish darted from some distance away and took the worm in its swift forward path, the line travelled and tightened. Robert easily controlled his puny catch and landed it on the bank. She laughed unkindly at it.

"Better than nothing," said Robert.

"It's not. You'll have to throw it back."

"It's big enough, just about."

"Oh, nowhere near, it's tiny. You know it's too little."

Robert extracted the hook, and gripped the fish in his hands. It flipped strongly.

"You're no fisherman if you keep that."

"I caught it, didn't I?"

"Whatever do you want it for?"

Robert had no answer. The fish arched itself frantically.

"You just want to prove something, to prove you can catch something. It's so young it doesn't know anything, you don't prove anything unless you'd caught the big one—"

"You didn't want me to."

"No, but if you had you'd be a good fisherman – I'd respect you even if I do hate fishing. I'd tell them at home, I'd even say I tried to scare him off. Anybody can catch little ones, they're for kids."

"I landed it."

"It just took the bait, you weren't trying for it."

"When you're fishing you're trying to catch a fish, stupid."

"You just had to land it to get the hook free, it got itself caught. You've held it, now put it back. You know you don't want it."

Obstinately he still held it tight. The poor thing opened its bleeding mouth pitifully.

"It'll die in a minute. I shan't say at home you caught a fish. I shan't say anything. You can show it to your father."

The fish was almost at its last gasp.

"You won't want to show him. He'll be angry, and Ron Evans will – Ron thought you were a proper fisherman. And I did, I'll never come with you again."

"Big deal!"

Her eyes were hot and sharp with tears. The little fish lay limp in Robert's hand.

"What a baby, crying for a fish!"

"I'm not. I'm crying for . . . because . . ."

She couldn't say why. But something she knew suddenly found its only expression in loud childish sobbing. Robert went to the water's edge and flung the fish as far as he could. It disappeared with a small splash.

Gradually, as the hard lump in her chest eased and melted, her tears ceased. She heaved a big sigh. Robert sat down without speaking and unwrapped what was left of the sandwiches. Presently she sat down beside him and together they finished them, and the lemonade.

"D'you want to have a go for him?" asked Robert. "You see Mister Big 'uns back again. D'you want to try for him?"

She nodded. He got to his feet and baited the hook for her, in a short while she became as absorbed as Robert had been. She asked his advice but he didn't give her much. "He's a crafty bugger. I reckon we won't catch him in a hurry," he said.

The kingfisher flew down the river again, and almost immediately flew back past them – they both saw it. Presently she gave the rod back to Robert. They sat side by side on the bank, Robert just dangled the worm out of sight under the bank. A silent breeze sprang up, ruffling the river's surface at the farther side. The willows moved, trailing their sun-yellow fingers in the water.

"A bit of wind. Let's have some action," said Robert. He bounced his rod up and down in an amateurish manner, flicking the worm in and out of the water. He made her laugh, he was funny, fooling about. In one movement he looped the worm into the air and flipped it carelessly over at the big fish. She thought it landed right on him.

With an incredible outraged turbulence of water in which he had lain so still for so long, he flashed up, showering spray from his galvanized body. Robert couldn't believe it. He leaped up too, nearly dropping the rod. Both the children were desperately excited. She screamed in surprise, clapping her hands, jumping up and down, and Robert's hands shook as he began to reel in: it was a bigger fish than he had ever caught before.

"What if he gets away! Oh, don't let him!" She chewed her fingers, she was sweating. So far, the trout was still hooked. "What if he breaks the line?" Robert was sweating too.

The tip of the rod bent to the water, the woodpecker rattle of his reel clocked up a timeless period of suspense. Robert drew his catch relentlessly closer, and closer till he judged the time was right and swung the big fish up in a triumphant arc on to the bank.

"Oh Robert, if you could see your face!"

"And yours!" He grinned at her. They were both crouching by his panting catch. A huge confidence born of success out of failure wrapped them both in unutterable content.

"He's swallowed the hook right down."

"Can you get it out?"

"Sure." While she waited for Robert to unhook the fish, the wind swayed in the willows again and the river seemed to be coming alive. Many fish were growing active; several rings appeared on the surface. She imagined the urgent upward fling of solid bodies made light in the water by a strange compulsion. Robert came and stood by her.

"He's heavy. I reckon he weighs a pound and a half, maybe."

"Look at them jump! They must feel so light and cheerful to jump like that."

They could clearly see many fish darting and gliding the length of the loop.

"Something gets to them," said Robert.

"The rings only show where they've been – not where they are now."

"They're all over the bloody place."

"I wonder what it is that gets to them."

They didn't feel like going home. Robert took a fresh worm. He had some luck, he had several stricken and landed two more fish. She watched him; watched the fish swimming; watched the willows and the river. She went a little way along the bank, took her sandals off and played about in the water. She crouched on the rocky floor of a small pool fringed with weed, where boatmen skated and a school of tiny minnows flickered.

The sun beat down upon her head and upon her neck, the breeze blew more strongly. She was conscious of no time but now, no place but here – the stream flowing cold round her bare feet might well have had neither source nor destination. This day might well have had no dawning, nor be approaching any nightfall.

Rob McColl (16)

We Are But Young

Please, just speak the truth to me
It's all I ever want to hear,
I beg you, no apology
My friend, you need give none to me,
Nor I to you, be but of cheer,
No empty jest or clever pun,
Our silence is no cause for fear.
For we don't need what's on your tongue,
These murmurings and words that run
Away from what the heart holds dear
Are but asides, your eyes are clear;
What can your enemies have done
That they seem to haunt you even here,
Where we are but fine friends, you and I?
I plead, enough of petty lies
When such good company is near,
Let us love and be as one
And let us not the fools despise
For who are we to criticize?
Instead let this strange smog be gone
That thickens dark and shadows sun,
These mantle mimes our feelings hide,
The breath of truth is whispering here
In wandering winds, the grasses sigh
With songs and sounds where silence lies.
And if you will a lonesome tear
Feel welling, it's all right to cry
For tears will sometimes clear the eye
Where the dirt of death has slowly dried,

Robert McColl (16)

And though the moon sees turning tides
The oceans see the years wash by
Neither to cease or drain and dry
And where the birds are soaring high
In lofty trees, in stormy skies
The timelessness of truth will fly;
Soft but sure the song is sung,
The honesty that we will die
And we'll know that light when that day comes,
Please no lies now, we are but young.
For now is here, and we are still young!

THE ROOM IS FULL OF QUESTIONS

Adam King (12)

Sarah Nelson (14)

Learning Early

My client has just walked in – he looks a wreck. Apparently, he is terrified of flying. He wants some kind of miracle cure. I pity him. I can't just utter some magic words, pop him on a plane and, hey ho, he's cured. I'm a psychiatrist. People come to me to find the answers to their problems. I can't do that. They have to find their own answers, just as I found mine.

I didn't always want to be a psychiatrist. I went through stages of wanting to be a policeman, an astronaut, a helicopter. I had always been an imaginative child. Becoming a psychiatrist had never even entered my mind.

I was never one to give answers. I used always to question. I would always ask hundreds of "What if?" questions. They were all highly unlikely and totally improbable, but I asked them nonetheless because I really, honestly wanted to know the answers. I would ask questions like, "What would you do if I withdrew one thousand pounds from my bank account and demanded it all in one pence pieces, then counted it all out there and then in case they'd short-changed me?"

A lot of people ignored me when I was younger and obsessed with questions. At school I only ever had one good friend, Jeremy, but even he got tired of my incessant queries.

I glance across at my client. He's staring at me, questions beginning to form on his lips:

"Can you help me? Will I ever overcome my fear? What can you do?"

I look away from his piteous face, and remember my own

immature desperation for answers. I remember my school, Jacob and Mortimer County First School.

I am in a huge hall, swarming with children. They, like myself, are clad in grey shorts and a light blue shirt. I am sitting cross-legged on the wooden floor, my friend Jeremy at my side. We are in the assembly hall, and prayers are being recited. The hushed whispers gradually diminish and I am left with the shouting inside my head. What would the silent teachers and children do if I stood up and screamed at the top of my voice, "I'm a bird, I can fly"? What would they do if I took off around the room? I turn and pose the question to Jeremy. He shrugs it off and whispers back "I'd ignore you I s'pose." I doubt very much that he would. I really want to know what he would do – what everyone would do. I need to know.

The hall is silent except for the monotonous drone of the Headmaster reading out a never-ending prayer, and the gentle hum of fidgeting little boys. I need an answer. "What would you do?" I feel myself stand. I'm no longer bored or tired, but very excited. I see hundreds of heads bent in prayer. I hear a voice, clear as a bell, shout out six words.

"I can fly; I'm a bird".

Everyone's heads jerk up and scan the hall for the voice that has interrupted their tedious world of prayer. I too look, and as I hear the phrase repeated, I realize that hundreds of eyes are fixed on me.

I begin to sweat and my uniform provides scant protection from the sea of burning eyes. I close my eyes and everyone disappears. My arms rise up and down at my sides and for a moment they are the downy wings of a bird. Around me the silence turns to murmurs and I realize that this is reality. This is my question and nobody is answering. But my question is not yet complete.

My scuffed-sandalled feet begin to take me slowly around the hall, getting faster and faster 'til I feel as though I'm flying. I am racing around the crowded hall where the once-silent, praying children shuffle about to clear my path. I can hear the stamp of my feet and a deafening throb of voices.

"What is he doing?"

What am I doing?

"Is he mad?"

Of course I'm mad!

Then, suddenly, I realize the answer to all my questions. Questions. The answer to "What would you do if?" is a question. They would ask a question.

Now I know the answer. I know all the answers and everyone else knows nothing.

"What is he doing?"

I know. You don't.

"Is he mad?"

I know and I'm not going to tell you. I won't tell you a thing. I've found my answer; you can find yours.

I calmly weave my way back to my vacant place and sit down. Jeremy stares, open mouthed.

"Don't worry," I whisper to him. "I know now."

Everyone is talking and walking around. Asking. Asking questions. The room is full of questions. I am the only one not asking. I know their questions and I know all the answers. Won't tell anyone my answer. Ever. I start to smile and continue to pray.

My client coughs and I am back in my office. He looks weary and tired of my silence. I stand up.

"I'm sorry," I tell him, "I'm afraid I can't help you," and I see him to the door.

Emma Morning (16)

*In Deep Water

In deep water I used to panic,
Thrashing wildly,
Gripped by the thought of the unfathomable
Uncertainties surrounding me,
Threatening to engulf me.

Striking out recklessly into bizarre provinces,
I would grab at any flotsam and jetsam that bobbed before my eye.
Straws to be clutched at,
Clichés to be mouthed,
Opinions to be borrowed.

Now as life floods in,
I try to swim more easily.
Moving with the currents,
Harnessing the surges,
Expressing myself with fluency.

Only occasionally does the old fear return:
The foot searching blindly for ledge or sandbank,
Fingers scrabbling for handholds,
And eyes darting for sanctuary.
Only then do the turbulent streams,
Carry me, unavailing, towards inaccessible, distant shores.

Rob McColl (16)

Final Thoughts

Together we might have lain by the slumbering willow
gazing in harmony beyond the slow-slipping heavens,
the breathing fields, the splash of stream water,
and soft in summer sun, wandered in woodland,
or warm in the wintertime, cradled in the cold.
Yes, warm in the joy of the sesaons we'd walk,
unfettered and found as one all-embracing love.
But dreams like the seasons, are born and will die
and the storms where I stumbled, they drowned out my
cries.
We might have danced freely in meadows in moonlight
or touched, as snow melted to drops on your skin
or scamped in the rain, beneath raging dark skies
in solace, your beauty like stars in the night,
the wild winds in your hair, your face and your eyes.

Now the night, it is here
in this weeping wood
where I stand
alone
and that same strange wind has blown you far,
and though I saw a path wending its weary way to
somewhere else
from these shadowy glades, the shivering trees huddled thick
about,
I fall, and all I need to know, I know is here.

But I wandered in places where the sound seemed like clouds,
and those shores they were hidden, unholy and so unknown.
Then the tears welled and strangled my gut, until finally
they could be quelled no more and fell as rain
from sodden skies, as floods in fields, unyielding seas
and rivers cold that flowed and flowed
and washed my lonely body down.

And I shivered, young and old upon the frosted ground,
as winters turned colder the fire in the earth
and froze the soils beneath my skin.
I lay, and the crowd found a weeping wretch
to fling to furnaces singed with screams,
and laughter filled the air with poison,
manifested by my different sin
that I was outcast and not of them,
to scrounge and bay for blood with them
and laugh at love, then die with them.

Empty as a midnight train I fell upon the pyre,
but all else was a naked leaf falling in the season's chill,
softly as snowflakes inside the landscapes of my mind
and meant nothing, as love fell far away in the fire.

Oh, purge me that fire, those flames, my fears,
Oh, charge me with sorrow with your hatred and curses
and strike me then stone me, forget me and flee me,
alone, but a baby, a plague on my body,
on this worthless body, so alone and afraid
without you, without me, only hounds and their howls.

Oh, drown me my drink, your eyes, my tears,
Hide me my hands, my heart, my hood
until the time I come to cast you off
and stumble on in my search no more
for candles in darkness and blossom in winter
and stars in the water, wells dripping with raindrops,
and the moon in my coffee, the truth in my dreams
and ships on horizons where the sun's sinking low,
but to wait until it finds me here
and whispers to my ears, my mind and my soul.

Oh, take me far away my boat and my boots,
my books and this borrowed mind,
the blowing winds flying onward forever
where no one might reach me
and no one might teach to me tales of tragedy,
tales of terrors and crawling men
with bodies so broken and a world so diseased
of greed and corruption, and never to cease
the rivers of religion flooding forth, blood
swollen by hatred, confusion of sin
and souls sunk in solitude searching for ways to
themselves, to each other or for some kind of peace.
And the years and days roll irrepressibly by
while others bent backwards can do nothing but try to
drive to distraction the bones they embody,
but lost in their loneliness break down and cry, where
stranded in seas their time has no place
and their time in its pace, it is racing them down
and will chase their life's blood 'till the day that they die
pounding on in its honesty, never to cease.

Oh, never to cease
As the chains of my doubt and this pride strain to crack
the anger, the conscience I seek to appease
because I'm one of those sailors in storm shaken seas
and my visions of golden shores safely with God.
Now I wait for a chorus of songbirds at dawn
with yours yet to shatter, for pass they must do,
and I pray it mercifully to make you see,
you see, there's more than you thought there could be.

But now please forgive me my judgement, my will,
My words and my whims that prove I sleep yet,
And lose me my lantern, my laughter, my longing,
and leave me to waste me, and dying want not for me
and only when my footprints are finally washed clear
by waves and seas of scathing storms
and the sludge and the mud has engulfed their frail forms
set my feet out again to walk on from here.

Oh, face me my face, my foes, my friends
With your blows blunt my anger, my sadness, my doubt
and with your claws more poignant my pain.
Oh flood me my failings, this ego, this fool,
and strip me naked to each
bitter wind until, screaming,
I am free of confusion and
bludgeoned down in the blood
and bones, I scream no more at the
honesty of my mind.
And when the laughing, leering people
die to my broken body and
when my eyes are clear
and the swelling subsides, though
not forgotten the leering when it dies,

I'll stand again as a scrag of
skin and walk and talk again
without crutches and cry
for the world, though it is laughing
and lastly,
Find me my light, my love, my life
and I'll stop immutable, like the hills and
whisper goodbye to you and the past,
but it will be a fond parting
and I'll hope you'll remember me
for he that first loved you;
though that love may wane
it cannot die, it is here forever,
by you forever, in the midst of your pain.

Know that I'll love you and care for you
as the earth or He or life or love,
or whatever you may wish to name it
when you walk in meadows and sun-dappled woodland
astride of mountains, of moorland, and
sailing on rivers and pastures of peace.
That which you feel then is also something of me,
though I'll have learnt to love again
for the sighing tides turn, yet the oceans remain,
and though the tides turn, the oceans remain.

Francesca Harris (15)

*Cancer

Dislike,
Mislike,
Lack of enlightenment,
Way of the crab – sideways.

Crust dwellers,
From the dark side of the sun,
We follow the way of the crab,
And elope with our shadows
Our lives governed by horology.
She is a strict master,
But God is unisex.

Four dimensions –
We have true command of only three,
But the fourth has a casting vote
And lives to serve a fifth.
Yet the fifth must yield to a sixth –
The ultimate challenge.
I will not wish to shake hands
With the final guest,
So I will follow the way of the crab
And attempt to elude him.

Postnote – backwards
forwards
sideways
time
love
age

Daniel Lester (16)

Three Recurring Minutes

He bowed his head and pressed his collar tight,
A shield against a shower of driving rain
Which, caught in steely lamplight, glanced, repelled,
From roof and sign and awning, once again
To fall, as dreary torrents until quelled
By paving stones or facades of shop fronts.

From out of shelter, now, a doorman shunts
The stranger, who moves on; his gaze is cast
Upon the festive shops, whose bright displays –
Like private homes – remote with doors shut fast,
Shine out upon the street, with lights ablaze,
But give no cheer at all to those who pass.

Ahead a cab draws up on street of glass,
A girl decants, excited by the rain
Or by some unheard joke. Her laugh is bright,
Her lover holds the door, her Titian mane
Warms up the street, caught in the golden light
That now floods out to tempt – convivial, sweet,
And bear them in from off the windswept street.

* * *

And the window of the restuarant gives a view,
Of the lovers with the friendly *maitre d'*
Passing tables laid for four and laid for two . . .
And a table meant for two with only she
Who is startled, hopeful, sad, then turns away.

For he still has not arrived and her dismay
Makes her glance down at her watch – she knits her brow –
And the waiter soon appears and once again
Asks her whether she will order something now,
So she quietly slips away into the rain,
Where her sense of isolation is less keen
Than it had been in the happier social scene.

* * *

Though she took the same route that a minute before
Had been used by the stranger, their paths would not meet,
For the only poor creature the young woman saw
Was a tramp bedding down for a night on the street,
Stuffing newspaper into his jacket for heat.

With a bin liner wrapped round his ankles and feet,
When at last he is settled and curled in a ball,
Those who pass by his doorway are hardly aware
That the bundle of rags there is human at all.
Except for a streetcar's occasional glare,
Now the street is deserted and still, save the sight
Of the persistent neon's intermittently bright

All-Nite . . . All-Nite . . All-Nite . . .

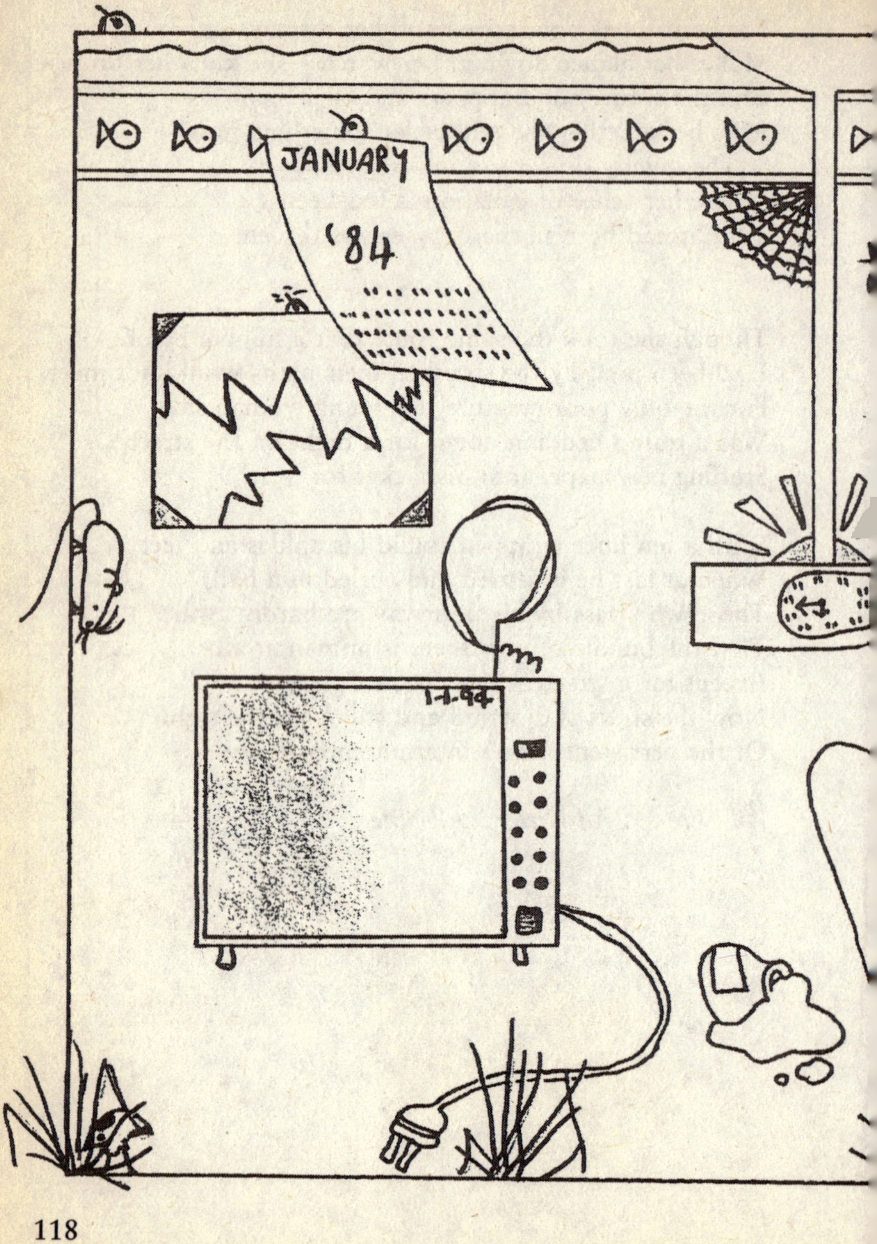
JANUARY
'84
1-1-94

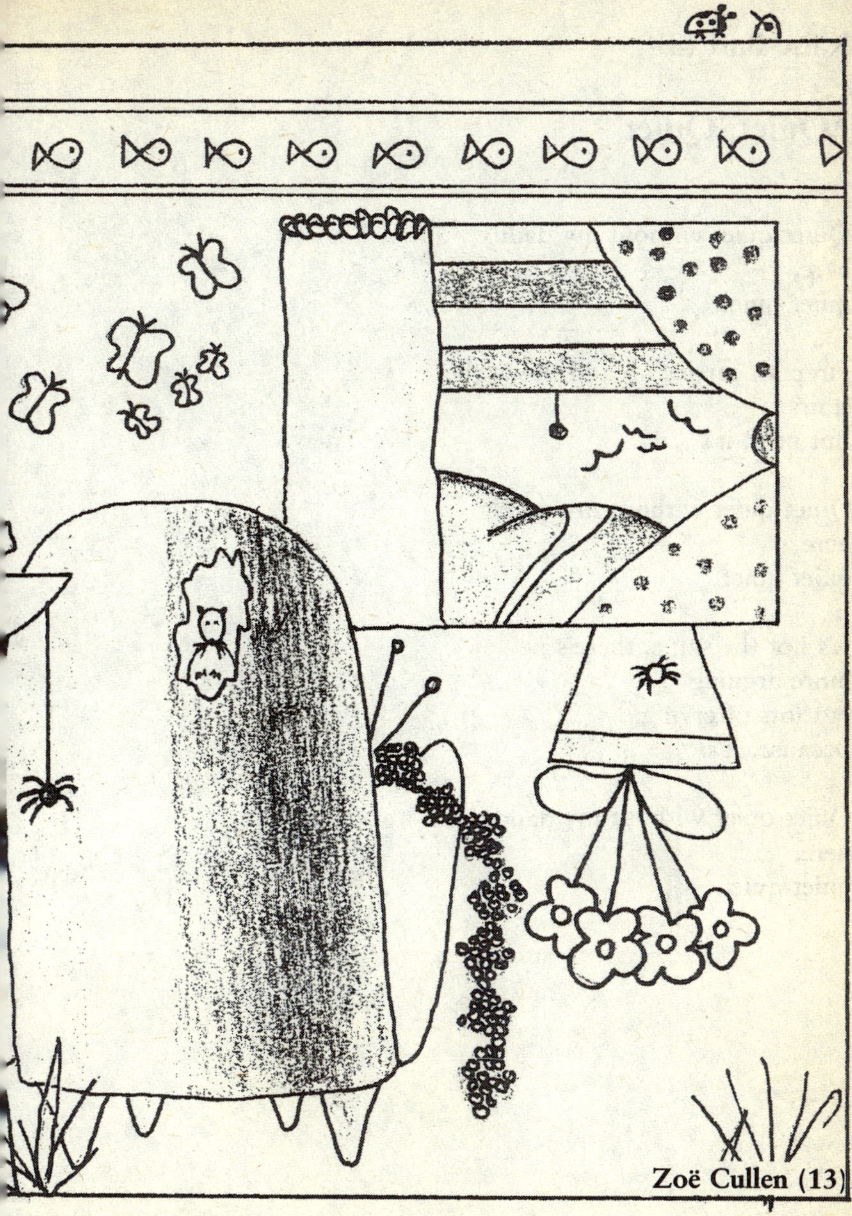

Zoë Cullen (13)

Katie Burt (8)

*Quiet, Quiet

Quiet quiet without my daddy
here,
quiet quiet.

Fireman carries up and down the
stairs.
But now, it's . . .

Quiet quiet without my daddy
here,
quiet quiet.

It's not the same, there's no
more arguing
but lots of crying.
Because, it's

Quiet quiet without my daddy
here,
quiet quiet.

Robert Hill (10)

*The Mirror

I glare into
The face of anyone
who comes into
My territory,
Whatever they see,
I am not lying,
I always tell the
Truth.
I ambush people's feelings
and faces.
At night
All I see is black!
Until morning when I
Once again start
From the beginning.

Sarah Goodall (8)

Nicholas Shopland (14)

*Keeper

The weather was surprisingly mild for October, and Bailey had no objections to driving up the stony track to the copse a little later than usual, even though the delay had been caused by another interview with the man, Carter, who usually put him in the worst of moods. At this time of year, however, the farm manager's infuriating assistant could do little to dampen Bailey's enthusiasm for the approaching first shoot; the annual prospect which provided all the justification Bailey needed to carry on. The green lane, its mossy banks stretching steeply several yards above him, provided the base for a tunnel of trees looming over the track, blocking out more and more of the faint moonlight. The darkness was instead intruded by the headlights of the vehicle as it jolted up towards the wood.

The track continued well up into the copse, but Bailey pulled into a gateway and left the Toyota pick-up out of sight before taking his double-barrelled shotgun under his arm, instructing Vic to jump down from the back of the vehicle, and picking up the bucket of barley. Carter wouldn't let him have wheat grains for reasons of cost-efficiency, and the gamekeeper was reminded, with an invasive bitterness, of their conversation earlier that evening as he began walking the rest of the way to the pen. Vic, his seven-year-old spaniel, trotted along beside him, but the old man paid little attention as he cast his mind back over the evening's events.

Carter had arrived just as Bailey was about to leave at around seven, a seemingly calculated effort to disrupt the keeper's routine, and having got his foot in the door, stated that he needed to talk about Bailey's wages. Bailey had attempted to terminate the proceedings immediately, but the younger man was of stronger will and voice, and they moved into the old man's sitting room. While Bailey poked at the already dying embers in his fire, Carter made his unreasonable demands in a particularly condescending, reasonable way. Now the gamekeeper's workload had been lessened, the farm could not realistically be expected to pay the same wage, and although he could remain in the tied cottage, Bailey's income would have to be cut quite significantly. Bailey, in righteous indignation, had thrown Carter out, the latter saying he would leave and return when the other was in a more receptive mood.

Bailey arrived at the pen and began whistling in order to call the poults in for feeding. Some of them had already gone to roost, and it took a full ten minutes of short, wavering whistles to call them together when he began scattering the grain about the area.

Bailey knew his shoot well, and he slowly realized that not all the four hundred or so birds were present. Amongst the large groups he could see no trace of the one cock with significant white streaks on its breast, nor could he see the bird with the red speckles on its white neck. More alert now, he walked quickly through a group of birds towards the fence surrounding the pen, where he fancied he saw a hole. Closer examination revealed a clear gap where the fencing had been dug and clawed away, and with an angry curse he turned to see the shredded remains of the white-breasted cock, and several hens, discarded by the vermin whose blood-lust was greater than its jaws. In the dim moonlight shrouded almost entirely by the towering ash trees, he could see an untidy path left by the animal too foolish to cover its own tracks. Bailey blinked, as if to trap the view on film, before turning and striding purposefully back through the copse towards his parked vehicle. His bewildered dog followed, steering clear of its master, who had stopped and thrown the remaining contents of the bucket on to the soft soil, before kicking them viciously ahead of him, showering his path with grain and loose earth. Picking up the bucket, Bailey continued towards the vehicle.

He returned an hour later without the dog, but with a large iron device under his left arm, and his shotgun hung downwards under his right as before.

The birds had dispersed, and he was left alone as he trod towards the untidy track left by the fox. He followed the trail some way into the wood then stopped, crouched low down by the track, and took out a torch from his coat pocket. He placed his shotgun on the ground, and switching on the torch and leaving it glaring into the trail in the earth, placed the closed iron structure across the path. Judging twice the size accordingly, he removed the trap, and took out from the "poacher's pocket" on the inside of his coat, a hammer with a hoe-like end behind the head. With this he dug away a shallow hole in the soil, throwing the twigs and stones surrounding it into a small pile beside him. When the dip was complete he once again took the trap, and with the confident but careful ability of an expert, clasped hold of the gin across the spring with his callused, dirty hands, and pushed the spring down against his knee, releasing the jaws. He then deftly positioned the flap against the plate with one hand, and laid the trap with a stick touching the jaw and the underside of the plate to prevent it snapping closed as he positioned it in the hollow. A short chain led from the gin to a metal stake which he hammered firmly into the ground a short distance from the trap itself. Bailey carefully removed the stick, replaced the hammer in his "poacher's pocket", and took out a miniature sieve. Into this he scooped a handful of fine soil, which he then sprinkled lightly over the open trap. He finished by scattering the stones and twigs around the trap, then stood back from the trail and surveyed his handiwork. His wrinkled lips twisted into a satisfied smile that was really more of a snarl, and he stepped back amongst the trees, brushing soil over his tracks with his worn leather boots until he was several feet from the trail. Again he blinked to engrave the trap's position on his memory, before turning away and walking back to his pick-up and driving home.

Bailey's house was characteristic of a tied cottage. If he cared enough, he could have made it appear to be well above his means, it being quite large with a thick thatch, an attractive fireplace, and some fine oak doors. However, the cottage resembled little more than a large shed: the rooms were sparsely furnished, with old mats almost worn through with years of heavy boots trodden over the faded patterns, and the curtains were generally left closed, or opened, for weeks at a time, and had not been replaced in forty years. In the kitchen the sideboards were coated with grime, and the electric oven was left unused, all food being prepared on a tiny stove in the corner.

The fireplace with its ornate mahogany mantlepiece, was the only feature of the sitting room which was not ignored. Once the ashes from the previous night had been swept into a bucket by the side of the hearth and the fire relaid, Bailey would polish the wooden border and mantlepiece which served as a bookcase for his scant library, meticulously removing and replacing each book in turn, and choosing one to flick through for half an hour before going into the copse for the morning's tasks.

When he returned that evening, he crossed the sitting room floor, and gazed along the spines of his scriptures: *Practical Trapping of Vermin and Birds*, *Confessions of a Poacher*, *The Gamekeeper at Home*, and several other volumes, all of which Bailey had read from cover to cover many, many times. What he hadn't learnt from those volumes of the nineteenth century, he had been taught by his father, and until he was ten years old, by his grandfather, who had then died from tuberculosis. Bailey held the experience of generations of gamekeeping in his blood, a concept rejected perhaps by recent scientists, but blindly accepted by his generation and those before him. Above the mantlepiece was a collection of glass cases containing a wide assortment of gamekeeping paraphernalia, ranging from several powerful rifles to a few stuffed birds. In the midst of this collection was a space, which until that evening had been occupied by a device outlawed many years previously. Bailey stared at the space, before drifting away in his creaking armchair to a fitful sleep.

He awoke early in the fresh autumn morning, shivering. Slowly the old man straightened up, blinked and gently shook his head, before glancing once again at the space above the fireplace. His eyes took on a new gleam, and he walked with increasing pace outside to his shed. He climbed into the pick-up a few minutes later with his shotgun, a U-shaped hay-fork, and a gruff command to his dog, who bounded up into the back of the vehicle which started up and pulled slowly out on to the track, before continuing up towards the copse for the third time in twelve hours.

Bailey did not know what he expected to find. Had he thought for any great length, he would have recognized the very small chance of anything being caught in the gin in only a few hours, but the mere possibility enthralled and excited him, and he allowed the pick-up to intrude the timeless area near the pen in his haste to reach the trap. Besides, it would be out of sight once he was properly in the wood.

As he came closer to the trap, the gleam in Bailey's eyes spread over his face, which became subtly contorted as every muscle in his body tightened a little. A thrill he had not experienced for many years began throbbing in his chest, and the arm with the shotgun hung over it became taut and shifted position as he grasped the barrel with his hand, the other hand clasped tightly on to the fork-handle. The increasing snarls and whimpers of Vic, restrained only by fear of his owner's rebuke, drove Bailey's excitement further, an excitement which peaked as he realized Vic's growling was being accompanied by that of his quarry. The fox came into sight and howled with furious terror as it leapt up, bringing the gin with it, the flat teeth gripped on its left hindleg, before it was held back by the chain, which was driven hard into the ground a foot behind the trap. Bailey's spaniel snarled and leapt for the fox, and it was a full five seconds before the growling pierced Bailey's stupor, and he shouted and brought the base of the hay-fork down on to the howling dog's back. When this was repeated the spaniel fell away, whimpering, Bailey turned his attentions to the bloody, drooling fox. He dropped the shotgun, and, holding the hay-fork tightly with both hands, advanced on the fox, which lunged forward in terror. Bailey swung the fork and clouted the fox sideways, then recovered his position and brought the U-shaped prongs down on either side of the fox's neck. With each yelp the old man thrust the fork deeper into the soil.

For a second he almost relented, but the sight of the fox's bloody jaw and the memory of the shredded carcass of the white-breasted cock commanded him to finish the task, and he took the hammer from his "poacher's pocket" and clubbed the fox's nose with the handle once, twice, three times, and many more after the animal was silenced. For a long time after he had straightened up he stood there, glaring at the fox's splintered skull. Vic's whimpering awoke him, and he walked over to his dog and stroked it roughly along its bruised back. As he turned to pull the hay-fork from the ground and reclaim the trap, he felt a shameful nauseous twinge, and turned away once more. When he turned back he looked only at the top of the fork-handle, which he grasped and pulled, now with very little strength, and felt the fox's head slide out from between the prongs. He would get the gin later. Still without looking he kicked the limp body into the trees, hidden from sight, then turned, and croaked a command to Vic who followed him, with only slightly wavering obedience.

Several yards away, a figure previously concealed behind a tree stepped out on to the path made by Bailey and his dog. Carter looked down at the remains of the fox and the iron jaws clasped around its hind leg, and, after a lengthy pause, followed the same trial his gamekeeper had taken.

Bailey noticed the footprints that evening when he went to reclaim the trap, and observe the fox's remains with his usual coldness. He surveyed the tracks with a grim smile. He would have to deal with this, and already he could see his actions beginning to catch up with him. It seemed strangely ironic that he should lose the total control he had for a few moments seemingly possessed. However, Bailey did not dwell on these problems; the important issue was the rapidly approaching first shoot, and the protection of the fowl until then. That evening, he flicked through the pages of *Confessions of a Poacher*, and rapidly ascertained how this particular vermin could be most effectively dealt with. Once again he looked up from his armchair to the wall above the fireplace, where the gleaming iron trap was hung once more amongst the glass cases, but he knew that this time the gin trap would be ineffective. But before he could get up to collect together the equipment needed, fatigue carried him away for another six hours.

The morning arrived, with none of the sparkle of the previous day; the sky had become obscured by towering grey clouds with dark, saturated bases, and by midday a few specks of rain began to land between the leaves of the canopies above Bailey, who was unloading a lengthy cloth bundle from the back of his pick-up. With his shotgun hung under his right arm as always, and the bundle under his left, he made his way into the wood towards the trail, though he kept away from the site of his skirmish with the fox. Kneeling down in the earth between two trees, he unwrapped the bundle and took out a roll of thin wire and a single-barrel shotgun, then rolled up the cloth and placed it in his "poacher's pocket".

As he worked, Bailey remained unaware that Carter was watching him from behind a nearby ash. When he was finished, he straightened up, and started to walk away. Carter stepped out too soon, and the noise of his tread brought the gamekeeper wheeling around to face him.

"How long— " the keeper began.

"Just coming through, Mr Bailey," Carter explained, glancing at Bailey's shotgun, "Just going for a walk."

Bailey eyed the man suspiciously, and shifted his grip on the barrel of his gun.

"Sorry I startled you," Carter added, sensing it wouldn't be enough. His eyes widened as the gamekeeper broke open his shotgun, and took two cartridges from the leather loops on his belt and fed them into the barrels before snapping the gun closed, bringing it up to chest level, and striding forwards towards the now terrified Carter. Ignoring Carter's stammered pleas, the old man continued to walk towards him until the assistant manager was cowering almost directly in front of him. Carter squealed and closed his eyes as two shots hammered through the wood in rapid succession, sending a dozen pheasants flapping out of the trees, piping in alarm.

A shower of twigs quickly persuaded Carter to open his eyes and see the keeper swing his shotgun downwards and break it open, the two spent cartridges springing on to the ground behind him. Stuttering wildly, Carter looked up at the remains of a nest, then down at the ground to see the shattered remains of a crow, peppered with shot. He looked up to see the gamekeeper making his way back through the copse, his shotgun hung under his right arm. Several minutes passed before Carter could follow him. The rain was now falling quite heavily.

The evening arrived and brought with it a strong wind and

an overcast sky. The rain had been falling hard for several hours, and Carter ran into the farm offices from his Range Rover holding his coat up over his head. He turned to the office secretary with a twisted smile of satisfaction.

"I think I've found fair grounds for Mr Bailey's dismissal," he remarked, and went through to his office, before removing his dripping coat with a flourish and picking up the telephone from his desk.

Bailey's shoot was only part of the wood which stretched out above and alongside the hills of the neighbouring farms and continued for several miles towards the coast. Bailey stumbled over the wooden fence into the sloping field from below the swaying trees, and stood against the raging force of the wind and the continual battering of the rain on his weathered face, his dog trotting to his side and sitting by his leg. From where he stood he could usually survey the land ahead for several miles, as he had done many times as a young boy with his father. Normally he could see not only the grassy fields below him but also the river ahead and the hills on the other side of the valley. On a clear day he could see the common beyond them, and on rare occasions he had fancied he could see the highest peaks of the moorland thirty miles away. But on this occasion the darkness and the storm hid the view from him, and, seeing no reason to remain, he began to make his way steadily down the saturated, grassy slope towards his cottage. The spaniel began to follow, but lost track of his master as other fascinating scents were unearthed by the storm and carried him back into the wood.

An hour later Bailey returned to his cottage and lit the feeble fire in the sitting room before sliding into his armchair with a painful grunt, and drifting slowly away once more. As he slept he did not see the unshaded low-watt bulb that had dimly illuminated the room suddenly go out, as nearer the farm a tree was battered down on to a power line. Only the occasional rolls of thunder could drown out the relentless moaning of the rain, which pervaded Bailey's dreams and caused his sleeping body to twitch and groan in the chair.

In the copse Vic scampered along an invisible path, head down, his stump of a tail wagging uncontrollably, oblivious to the commotion around him. As he followed the trail towards its source, the spaniel's nose touched a thin wire, stretching it across his face.

The gunshot and the fluttering confusion of startled pheasants that followed it were inaudible outside the wood, such was the tremendous bellow of the wind that now seemed intent on destruction. Higher up, the loose soil at the top of a slope gave way as the roots of a tree were ripped out of the ground, and a torrent of stone-filled water rushed down from the wood over the hills and down into the stony track, which was quickly torn apart leaving several rushing gullies running down towards the valley base. In the copse itself, the roots of a silver birch failed to hold it in the ground and it toppled on to its neighbour, bringing the two slender trees down on to Bailey's pen. As the canopies of the wood were blown wildly about, the scattering of Bailey's poults into a mad flight was accompanied by another burst of thunder.

Bailey was awoken by a heavy knocking. He could only see by the glowing embers of his fire, and he stood up carefully before walking with an unusually awkward gait to his window. The storm was still raging outside, and the old man gazed through the glass into the glare of two headlamps distorted by the raindrops on the glass. In this light he could just distinguish the white car, and could almost read the large blue lettering on its side, though there was little point. With a sigh of resignation the old man straightened up, turned, and began moving slowly towards his front door.

Jonathan Petch (16)

A Successful Judgement

Voices drifting away. Light being obscured by clouds. Everything fading into nothingness, and then – blackness.

The stout, red-faced man opened and closed his eyes, but there was no change. All around lay blackness, nothing else. He tried to move, but only succeeded in spinning slowly in an indeterminate direction. He appeared to be floating in nothingness. The Void. The man tried to call out, but there was nowhere for the sound to carry to. He realized with a start that he had not been breathing for some time. How long, he could not tell. Seconds, or hours? Or years? Time didn't appear to exist in this place, wherever or whatever it was.

He tried to think of his last coherent memory. He couldn't breathe, couldn't speak, could hardly move, and all he could do was think. Just think . . .

Memories drifted back to him: vague faces, dimly recalled events. He remembered a dinner, a big hall and faces he knew near him, acquaintances of his. He was eating, talking, laughing at conceited jokes, flaunting his money and masculinity to the ladies. Then . . . there had been a sudden, stabbing pain in his heart. It felt like it was exploding and imploding simultaneously . . . and now this. Something clicked, and everything abruptly fell into place. Then one thought solely filled it all, and the magnitude of this left him floating stunned, as if he were dead. It generally comes as quite a shock when you realize that this is exactly what you are.

After an infinite age he started to recover what little composure he had left. Nothing had prepared him for this. Of all the stress therapists he had ever seen, none had give advice on coming to terms with your own death.

"So this is heaven," he thought. "Hmmm . . . it's a bit dark."

He looked into the utter blackness and frowned, his plump face crumpling up in great worry lines like a newspaper. Then something caught his eye: one pinprick of light, an indefinite distance away. The man suddenly felt some obscure, intangible sense of waiting somehow, as if he was gradually, painfully, slowly floating towards the minuscule light that was the only feature in the emptiness. It reminded him of waiting in the queue at the hypermarket.

"Aha, we're not in heaven yet, but we will be soon."

The man felt relieved that the Christian beliefs that he had never doubted during his lifetime were being proved so true. He was in a strange way feeling vaguely triumphant. He knew that there would be no problem with him getting into heaven, not after the virtuous life he had led on earth. And what a life he had had, he considered proudly, rewinding the video of his moments of glory. Think of all the good things I have done, what successes I have had! And then, of course, there was his insurance policy; he had always, well usually, gone to church on Sundays, always knelt and mumbled prayers with the minister. And he always crossed himself before signing a new business deal, not, of course, because he didn't have complete faith in his skills as a businessman, just to make sure that all the money he donated to the church was being put to appropriate usage.

Although he had never really got round to reading the Bible, he had vague ideas that you had to have led a good and successful life to obtain your visa for the Pearly Gates. He could claim to be a Christian anyway, so he couldn't foresee any problem. Indeed, he was quite looking forward to this heaven place, where all whims and desires could be satisfied . . .

Reminiscing over his life, he considered just how successful he viewed it to be. He had been the manager of dozens of production lines within the company distributed all around the globe. The man's most profitable and successful venture had been the opening of a huge factory in Taiwan. If that didn't demonstrate his worthiness when judged, he thought, then what did? This factory had been the pride of the company had the envy of its rivals. He had even personally suppressed vital information that environmentalists could have seized upon and which would have drastically cut the profit margin; of course, under the unwritten rules of market forces the profit takes precedence over any pansy concerns about poisoned rivers. The man felt sure God would understand – he would probably have faced similar problems when he took out the contract to create Earth. And in any case, he employed thousands of foreign workers, all wearing their identical blue uniforms and caps, all taking their pay packets home to their wives and families, and all were happy. OK, the pay wasn't very much, but they looked content, or at least the man thought so. Anyway, who cares, he made a hell of a lot of money out of it, and if a man's wealth doesn't indicate his success, then what does? He had had almost everything he wanted on earth, and persuaded himself that he was kind and thoughtful towards other people . . . generally.

The light had been moving slowly but steadily towards him all this time, and now it was bright enough to see by. Looking down at himself, he noticed with pleasure that he was wearing his best suit, and looking smart and tidy. What an impression he was going to make on God, he thought, not like any of those scruffy whingeing greenies, who've never done a hard, money-making day's work in their lives. He prepared himself to meet his maker.

The brightness surrounded him, in complete contrast to

the dark that had encompassed the man for an indefinite period of time. Still, however, there were absolutely no features. This time, though, a sound could be heard which could be nothing but the scratching of millions upon millions of pens on paper . . .

Then a dull and despondent voice came from nowhere. From the two words it spoke, the man was able to determine more about the nature of the universe than he had ever done during his life. It was the most ridiculously bored voice he had ever heard. The man had been to boring office parties, but this voice sounded as though it had spent all eternity, if not longer, at the most boring office party ever held anywhere in the universe. God pronounced two single words:

"Unworthy. Next."

Blanche Mcintyre (12)

Robert McLachlan (16)

Deletion

It was a Wednesday. Syra knew it was Wednesday because Wednesday was his duty day at the Centre. The Centre was the huge information depository situated under the polluted water of the Atlantic. Like some distended spider, the underground leviathan sat at the centre of a web. Gigantic cables stuffed full of fibre optics spanned the still sea bottom, connecting the Centre with every country on earth. Small islands, insignificant, with perhaps only a hundred or so inhabitants, warranted perhaps a cable as wide as the little finger of a man. In contrast, the administrative giants of the United States of America and the European Community were connected to the Centre by huge straight tunnels, as thick as a tank.

Syra was in command of the Credit and Commerce department for England. This was a rare privilege, granted only to especially trusted individuals, and Syra had worked his way up through the ranks over a period of thirty years to reach the zenith of his department. He shared the post with seven other people, who were also specially screened. The department was necessarily secure, because the person in charge could have at his fingertips about a trillion pounds. However, Syra was not interested in that wealth. He knew that some of his colleagues judiciously siphoned off a few thousand pounds each time their duty came up despite the screening (after all, is anyone completely honest?) but not Syra. He was too interested in people and their day to day finances. When he was in front of that console in his office, he felt like a god.

With a few movements of his fingers, Syra could call up the credit profile of any person he wanted. He could then take away all their money or give them a fortune. Syra, however, was not compassionate or generous. He enjoyed deleting.

Deleting was a particularly drastic form of punishment – in fact, it was not now used due to the growing global pollution problem because it had a pronounced effect on your health as well as on your credit balance. It was not the removing of all money, it was the removal of the account. This was so drastic because on Earth, everything was paid for by the individual from the moment he was born. Air, food, water, education, healthcare were all things which debited selected amounts of money each and every day. If no money was forthcoming, then the services began disappearing. First education, then the long list of private utilities and finally air.

The Earth had been so badly mauled by the rigours of the twentieth century that the clean-up now starting (after colossal public protest) would only begin to have effect by the next century. Therefore the air outside was at best stifling, and all the air was passed through gigantic purifying plants before being released into the domed cities. This air naturally had to be paid for . . .

Syra had deleted about five hundred people. Most were hired killings by credit companies, unwilling to pay for their clients' lives. In another age, Syra would have been condemned as a mass murderer or shady assassin. In this era of capitalism, if you didn't have the money, your life was worth no more than that of the lowliest microbe if you were out of the public eye. His killings had not been noticed because the people were gone. They did not exist, and consequently were not noticed by any authority as having died. Their airless apartments were now haven for nothing except a corpse. Friends of those deleted did not voice their suspicions, being too afraid of the credit corporations to stand out. Those that did often ended up with a polite note from their company informing them that their account would be removed "in three days, following unacceptable insurance risks."

Syra had no qualms about deleting people. He regarded his job as very necessary and considered himself as a caring member of the community.

This particular Wednesday, Syra was browsing through the files and setting up cross-sections of the state credit files. He looked up the name of a person who he had met at a recent party. The result of the search revealed he was a publicity agent for UniCred, one of the largest credit agencies in the USA. "Damn," muttered Syra, as he had been hoping to delete the idiot. He cleared the screen, and accessed another file – his own. He smiled as he gloated over the credit balance displayed at the foot of the screen.

Reaching over, he switched on the television and picked up the remote control. He watched, bored, as people voted for a screaming man to be dropped in a vat of burning oil for answering a question wrongly, and added his own vote with the handset – "Yes", naturally. He switched off as the grinning compère swam into view, and got up to stand by the window.

Looking out on to the tearing waters of the Atlantic, Syra was interrupted by a knock at his door. "Come in," he said. The door opened, and Syra smiled as his girlfriend peeped around. She walked in, holding her hands behind her back. Syra folded his arms.

"Another present?" he asked.

"Just a small one, dear, I'm sure you'll like it – it's *very* expensive," she replied.

Syra wasn't really in the mood for surprises, but the mention of money made him happier. So he held out his hands. His girlfriend walked up to him.

"Close yor eyes," she said, "and wait." Syra did this, and felt a furry body being placed into his hands. He opened his eyes, and sitting in his palms was a small kitten. It looked up at him out of soft black eyes, and opened its mouth in a silent yawn, glancing around the room. He looked up at his girlfriend in amusement.

"Why, thank you dear," said Syra. "Where on earth did you get him from?"

"You'd never guess," she replied. "I got him from my brother – he owns one of the only pet shops in London, and this kitten is one of the very few of them in the world."

There was a silence as the kitten walked around Syra's hands. He bent down and put the small animal on the floor, pushing it away from them gently with his shoe. Syra retired with his girlfriend to the next room, leaving the kitten behind in the office.

The kitten watched them go silently, and then turned towards the chair, spying the soft cushion on the seat. It jumped up and nestled down in the heat where Syra had been sitting. Above it, the computer screen continued to show Syra's personal accounts. Presently the kitten got up, feeling hungry. At that moment, Syra and his girlfriend came out of the room, arm in arm and slightly flushed.

"Would you like to come back to my apartment for lunch?" asked Syra.

"All right, darling," said his companion.

Syra reached over to the door and retrieved his coat from the hook. He looked at the kitten.

"Should we feed that thing?" He asked the woman, naturally presuming her to be an expert in such things. The woman halted.

"I'm sure it will be all right for a day or so – I don't think they eat very much, anyway," she answered.

She actually had no idea, but had never seen her brother feeding the ones in his shop, so did not want to waste time contacting him to find out. The two companions left the office, turning off the lights and locking the door.

The kitten looked around, and opened its mouth, mewling plaintively to be fed.

A few hours later, the kitten was beginning to get unsteady and delirious. It jumped on to the chair, dimly illuminated by the computer screen. It looked up at the glowing display, thinking it a way out, and jumped up on to the desk. The glass screen did not look like a window, but the fatigued kitten could not see properly. It walked forward, and on to the keyboard. A succession of "M"s and "H"s cascaded across the screen, and the kitten stepped back, alarmed, pressing a function key. The screen went blank, and slowly printed a list of options to the uncomprehending eyes of the animal.

The kitten stepped forward again, pushing its face to the screen, and trying vainly to get out through the imaginary portal. Its paws scrabbled at the keyboard as it cried in frustration and hopelessness. The computer emitted a soft beep, and returned to the information screen. The kitten fell back on to the floor, landing heavily on its back. A trickle of blood dripped from its mouth and merged into the deeper red of the carpet as its small body stopped moving.

On the desk above, the computer was steadily working, emptying myriad databanks of all memory of Syra James Clarke, 008673f43a2.

In an apartment in the South of England, two people began to suffocate. Slowly.

TIME IS AN ICEBERG

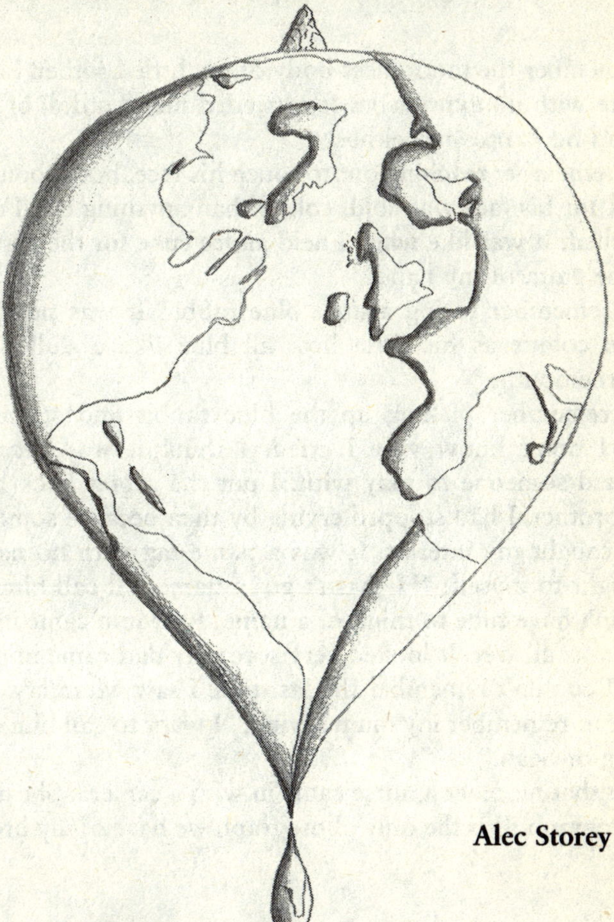

Alec Storey (11)

Nicola Peck (12)

Memories of my Brother

I remember the motionless body of my little brother, his face white with no expression. It reminded me of a doll of mine. It had no expression either.

I remember reaching out to touch his face, but I soon drew back for his face was cold, colder than anything else I'd ever touched. It was like when I held an ice cube for the first time in the palm of my hand.

I remember seeing a little blue rabbit. It was nearly the same colour as his little lips, all blue like a dull day in Bournemouth.

I remember picking up the blue rabbit and starting to cry. I don't know why I cried. I think it was because I wanted someone to play with. I put the rabbit back beside my brother. I had stopped crying by then because something else caught my interest. It was a name tag with no name. I thought to myself, "He hasn't got a name. I'll call him . . . " I didn't have time to think of a name, for Mum came in. Her face was all wet. It looked very sore. My dad came in beside her. I couldn't remember the last time I saw Mum cry.

I can remember my mum saying, "I want to call him either Craig or Sean."

At that moment a nurse came in with a camera. She took a photograph. It is the only photograph we have of my brother.

Danny Manning (11)

*The Climb

I watched the steam rising out of the bath. I was shaking like mad. I watched a spider climb the smooth wall. I flicked it off with my finger. It fell and hung from its silky thread, dangling in mid air, then quickly working its legs up the thread to the wall, to safety. Just before it got there, I broke the thread with the tip of my finger. The spider fell into the bath, struggled for a moment in the clear water and then floated there, limp, dead. I ground my teeth together and almost chickened out of it totally. I would have if the doorbell hadn't rung.

It was my friend John. He had his camera with him, so somewhat reluctantly I realized that he was serious about doing it. I climbed out of the bath and got dressed. I found it hard to put my clothes on. I kept on wondering whether these were the right things to wear. I suppose its only natural when you've got it in your mind that you might not ever change out of them again. I walked down the stairs. I was shaking so much I almost stumbled and fell. I had to get out of this mood. I had to stop shaking. If I couldn't walk down the stairs I definitely couldn't climb a cliff.

"Be back by lunch," said Mum as she shut the door.

"Be back by lunch," I repeated in my head. Those might be the last words I hear from my Mum. "Be back by lunch."

We didn't talk much on the way to the gorge. It was a good two miles. All the time we had been planning it we had talked non-stop. We'd discovered the blow-hole two months ago and ever since then I had been wanting to climb it. It was only last month that I decided I would, and every weekend since then we'd been planning the route, the day, the date, the time. It had taken ages. We used up two reels of film just taking photos of it to plan the route.

The tide was fully out now. It would be high at two. John was an hour late, but it didn't matter much. We had given ourselves two hours' flexibility. He had been buying film for the camera. He was going to photograph me climbing and put it in the school newspaper, and maybe even the local newspaper. But at the moment it was only me and him who knew about it. If anyone else knew, they would try and stop us. Especially if they knew we didn't have any equipment.

The thing I wanted most right now was for someone to walk over the hill and ask us what we were doing. Then it would all be over. I'd stop shaking and that tense feeling in my tummy would be gone. Finished, no cliff, no climbing, no excitement . . . disappointment. No, I didn't want someone to walk over that hill.

We reached the top of the hill. Suddenly I felt the wind. It almost knocked me over. It must have been around gale force. I could see that John sensed the danger but he didn't say anything. And then, there it was. The sea, Lundy Bay, a small sandy bay surrounded by cliffs. The blow-hole was on the left-hand side of the bay. It went right through the cliff and opened out into the sea.

I was aiming to climb from one side right over and down the other side. The first thing I looked at was the waves. They weren't too big. I could still do it. The wind didn't matter that much. It was coming from the north-west, and in the blow-hole that side is totally sheltered.

As we approached the beach I realized the waves were bigger than I had thought. A seagull swooped in with the wind. It flew over the hill; away, gone.

"Nasty waves," said John. "Probably splashes halfway up the blow-whole. Better be careful."

The tide was now on its way in. There was nobody down

at the beach, not that that was surprising. Most people don't go down to the beach at half past eight in the morning, especially if it's a two mile walk down to it. It somehow felt isolated, scary.

We went straight to the blow-hole. John had taught me all the moves I had to do. He started putting me through them again, talking me through them very briefly. He set up the camera at the top left-hand side of the blow-hole. There was a small climb down the actual blow-hole and then I would start it, beginning on the left-hand side, ending on the right. If I got there, I added in my head.

As a wave came in, it covered the rocks below. The foaming white water sent a chill down my spine. You wouldn't survive one wave. The waves were coming in slowly but strongly, about every seven seconds.

John told me what his plan was. He would first of all take the first shots from where he was, then he'd climb down a bit and take the rest of it from a ledge about half-way down. There was a giant shadow over the part I was climbing. I could hardly see my holds. This made me more nervous.

There was perspiration on my face, on my hands, everywhere. I wiped it with my T-shirt. John got out the chalk, and I rubbed it all over my hands thickly. He put the film in the camera and we were ready. I wanted to delay as long as possible but the longer I waited, the more dangerous it would be, as the tide was coming in fast. John kept on telling me (and I kept on telling myself) the climb should only last twenty to twenty five minutes – if I made it . . .

I started the descent down to the first ledge. I wasn't shaking any more. I seemed to only do it when I was standing still. I tested every rock by knocking it first. Some crumbled, some didn't. I tried to put the minimum amount of weight on each hold. I reached the ledge and breathed deeply. That part had been tricky and I hadn't even started climbing.

"OK down there?" shouted John.

"Yes," I shouted back, bravely; but I wasn't feeling it at all.

The first ascent up to the beginning of the overhang would take me seven to eight minutes, I thought to myself. Once I got there, I'd begin the hard part, going over the actual blowhole. That should take five minutes. Then I could have a rest. I decided I'd think about the next part once I was there. I knew the actual overhang would be hard. Well, it wouldn't have been easy for the most experienced climber, and I wasn't the most experienced climber, otherwise I wouldn't be here, not without ropes and proper equipment. I began to wonder why I was climbing this at all. It was my addictive passion for climbing. It was like a hungry monster wriggling around in my brain, and the problem was that when I fed it, it just got more hungry.

Quickly and quite clumsily I started, slipping down immediately. It was only then I noticed that the whole of the rock wall was covered in a slippery seaweed. I changed my handhold for a higher one that wasn't so slippery, and pulled myself up. It took me ten minutes to get to the top of the overhang. I looked across the gap between the two sides. The rocks looked quite crumbly. I carefully slipped my hand across the roof of the gorge to a small pocket which I could fit three fingers into. I wiggled my fingers about in the hole until they felt as comfortable as possible.

I breathed in deeply. My heart was thumping past. I shut my eyes for a moment but opened them immediately to dampen the picture of my limp body lying at the bottom of the gorge. I moved my jaw from side to side since that was the only part of my body I could move without slipping.

I set my eyes on the next handhold I would take, then looked back down to the side of the cliff. I ran my eyes along the gravel path which led down to a series of steps. John was perched just above this path at a point where the fence ended.

He looked back up at me, with a worried expression on his face. One hand was clenched to the rock-face and the other to the camera. He nodded his head slightly to one side to signal for me to go, but I just stared down at him for another few seconds. My mind was drifting from what I was doing to what could happen. A sharp call from John brought me back to reality.

"Go on then! You can't stay there for ever!"

His voice was shaking too, as if he was up there with me. Right at that moment I would have gladly swapped places with him.

I focused again on the next grip and prepared to swing out over the roaring waves. With one short rocking motion I lunged forward to grab at the other hold, but missed. I swung back but my hand wasn't secure and started to slip. I reached up with my other hand to support it, but the changing weight made me lose my grip even more. I tried to scream but the sound didn't come out. I was beginning to panic now. All my weight was on two fingers, and they were slowly sliding down out of the hold. For one split second I thought I was falling, and in desperation I frantically smashed my other hand against the rockface, trying to find a hold.

I don't know how I managed, but the next thing I knew, both hands were gripping tightly on to a curved piece of rock. My knees were tucked up to my chest and my right foot was stuffed in a small crack. For what seemed like hours I hung there, oblivious both to John's calls and to the deafening sound of the waves crashing against the rocks far below me.

I felt a warm trickle run down my face and on to my knee. I could see its shiny red surface as another droplet dribbled down. I felt like wiping it off but I was too petrified to move. Eventually I managed to get myself to turn my head and look down to where John was standing. As soon as I saw him, it was like switching the volume up on the television. The sea thundered in my ears, and now I heard John shouting up as well. I couldn't exactly hear what he was saying, but it was a comfort to hear someone else's voice.

I pulled my leg out of the crack, and reached up for the next hold. My paralysed body suddenly started working again, and somehow I found myself going from grip to grip until I reached the other side. A grin spread across my face as I reached the vertical face of rock. The worst of the climb was over. All I had to do now was go down, and I was finished. From this point it was impossible to see John or most of the path and fence. This also was when John was to climb down to the ledge below, where I would meet him.

The joy of finishing the overhang was tremendous. A moment earlier I didn't think I would reach this side, and now I was here. Everything had gone as planned. I looked out across the vast sea, right out to the horizon, and then up at the blue sky. From here the waves looked much more safe and less powerful, like small ripples on a lake. I gazed at the parts of the cliff I would never dare to climb, where there were precariously perched amazing nests of seabirds. I watched an adult gull fly into one of the cracks and out again, gliding across the open sea.

I started the easy descent down to the ledge. I was about a metre away from it when I peered out and saw John's face. He was holding his breath and although I couldn't see the rest of his body I knew he was in trouble. I hurried down and edged across towards him. He was clinging desperately to the rockface. He was panicking, even though the ledge was just like a small path. The height made him terrified. I bit my bottom lip. I reached out towards his hand, as a wave from below splashed against us. The camera slipped out of his hand. He grabbed at it and let go of his left hand.

"John!"

My voice echoed through the gorge, as with a sharp scream he plummeted down to land on a cluster of rocks about ten feet below me. Immediately I scrambled down to where his limp body was lying. His face was scrunched up and tears were pouring down his cheeks. He seemed in agony and didn't move at all. He muttered something about his leg.

"Can you stand up?" I asked, but there was no answer. He just lay there.

"Quickly, get up," I shouted at him, "please get up!"

His trusting face looked up at me. I had to get him out before the next wave came. Nervously I looked out to sea. I could see a large wave rolling in. I grabbed him by his arms and dragged him to the side of the cliff but he screamed with pain. The wave was just about to enter the gorge now. I had to get him some way up the cliff. I needed one hand for holding on myself, so I clutched him by the wrist. The surf was almost on us now. I grabbed at a ledge to keep myself steady, at the same time gripping on to his wrist as hard as I could.

I felt the pull of the wave on my hand as John was being dragged in. I held on as tight as I could. An icy shiver ran through my body, as John's hand slipped out of mine.

Alexandra Rogers-England (16)

*The Way Home

The sky is blue above me; an intense, hazy blue. It is not the dark angry bruise which spreads across the sky before a storm, nor is it the half-hearted forget-me-not wash of a children's art class. It is the blue of the French flag, of a field of cornflowers, a mediterranean sea. A warm, dusty blue. Bumble bees drone around my face. A big furry one bumps my nose. Other girls might scream, jump up, flap it away from them. But I am not other girls. That is the best way to get stung. Stephen told me that, as we sat on the grass behind my grandmother's house. He told me to stand still when dogs came bounding past – at six . . . huge dogs dripping fresh blood from six-inch fangs. Now, Yorkshire terriers and Scottie dogs. He showed me, patiently, how to skip. His sister taught him when she came over from Canada, the summer before I was five. He showed me how to bargain for comic books. He had the best comic books in his whole school.

The priest intones, "Ashes to ashes."

Lying flat on my stomach I can see the mourners gathered around the coffin. There are a lot of people. An old woman. Seven or ten ladies in black dresses. A little girl. A boy, nine or ten – from the back he looks like my brother. Men, in black three-piecers, uncountable, amalgamated by age. And the middle-aged women. Some in Laura Ashley, or BHS Funeral Range, and heavy-brimmed hats, others, in straw-blonde hair and belted black sacks. They look like uncles and aunts, cousins once removed.

Stephen said there was going to be a funeral at the Morrison estate.

"They're going to bury someone in the Morrison estate?" my brother asks. Stephen sighs.

"They're going to have the reception at the Morrison estate," he explains.

"What's a reception?"

"Honestly, Robert, don't you know anything? A reception is where they have food for the people at the funeral. It's because people have come such a long way, they don't want them to think it's just to see a coffin being lowered into the ground."

"Are we going to see it?" my brother asks, almost in a whisper. "Are we, Stephen? Can we? Please?"

"I don't know."

"Please?" I add my voice to my brother's.

Stephen chews his lower lip. "Not much to see, really. Just a couple of speeches, the will being read out."

"What's a will?"

"Oh come on, Robert, you must know what a will is."

My brother shakes his head.

"It's what a dead person leaves to stop the relatives squabbling over who gets what." Stephen shakes his head. "I don't know if we should go."

"Please, Stephen."

"It's not a party, Robert. We'll have to be very quiet. Very grown up," he adds.

The "we" is rhetorical. He is already grown up, he is almost twelve. He knows, and we listen to him. He has been to funerals before.

"So much grief in that boy's life," said my Aunt Hannah.

Miss Martin was there. Why had the Morrisons invited Robert's teacher? But Stephen explained. He told my parents and our grandmother, that we had got lost, we had been exploring. They believed him. It made our fumbling half-truths seem like the crudest deception.

Along the rusting railway track my brother pretends to be a train. Stephen and I follow behind, he is not even concealing his amused smile, he whistles and watches me. I am proving to him that I am grown up. The back of my neck hurts, the collar is over starched, my shoes are too tight, I am used to sneakers. I would rather be playing trains with Robert, or trying to walk on the jutting railway lines, tugging on the scratchy heather for balance.

Stephen has been teasing me. Not like he teases Julia and Rachel, he does not want to make me scream and run inside to my mother. Besides, thanks to him I am unafraid of spiders. He says I am immature. He tweaks my plaits, the plaits my mother likes me to wear to visit Stephen and Grandma. He watches me play hopscotch and wobble and fall way before I reach my marker. He laughs at me, he cannot believe I am almost nine, I am so childish. What do I do wrong?

"You can't do handstands. You can't jump off the big tree. You play trains." Only a baby plays trains.

He would still rather I didn't play dolls; tea parties with miniature china cups and plates. He is thankful I don't ask Grandma if I can "use the swing", like Julia and Rachel. "Teach me to do handstands then," I say. Later, my mother asks me why my legs are bruised.

My brother puffs. "Where are we going?"

We do not answer him. He repeats, "Where are we going?" Like a song, "Where are we going, Stephen and Caroline?"

We are almost at Aunt Hannah's house, we have passed over the bridge. And when I get there I will have won. I will be able to stop pretending. I will play trains on the way home, and Stephen will join in. I have learnt this about Stephen. He will not be left out.

The coffin is being lowered into the ground now, on long, white strips of cloth. A woman, young, blonde, begins to furiously stab her face with a white handkerchief. This is wrong, no one else is crying, and her dress is wrong too, short, seamed lycra, dull black and a little too big.

Earth is crumbled on top of the coffin, by a gerbil-faced man. I have an unpinnable feeling that he should be familiar. I like him. He is the kind of man I would marry.

Stephen is eighteen. I am unable to believe this, four years younger and balancing drinks through swaying crowds, in a green stretchy dress. I coast along the raised floor in my requisite three-inch heels, thrusting non-alcoholic wine at people I don't know. Boys from Stephen's school, their girlfriends, my grandmother's million aquaintances, who look more at home than my parents. In a corner, my brother and his cronies play cards for money. My brother plays viciously, as Stephen taught us to, every few minutes he gets up and trots over to my mother to put more money in the special pocket of her bag.

Aunts and uncles, distant cousins stop me. "Julia!" or "Rachel!" they cry. How I've grown. It was, er, Caroline who used to be the tall one, wasn't it? I smile, and nod, and answer questions about Caroline, who they hear is not doing too well at school.

I sit in a corner on the shell of an orange plastic chair. The light rock intensified with each passing adult and has now developed a heavy base beat which thuds into my head. My parents have gone, my brother's casino is empty. The harmony is jagged and colourful. Rachel has gone but Julia is giggling with one of Stephen's friends over in the corner. I feel too young. I should have accepted Grandma's lift. Who will take me home now? I will get home in the same mysterious way teenagers always do from parties. The bus is too mundane. Maybe I'll walk.

I can't see Stephen.

I have seen him only once tonight, before the friends arrived. He approved my clothes, said I looked cute.

Where is he? A drunken hulk lurches past, spraying sour beer and onions.

And I see Stephen, in the middle of a slowly beating throng. His starched collar is loose, his tie hangs from his shoulders. A cigarette droops from his mouth. He wears a slightly moronic smile.

I look at him until his eyes meet mine, and the smile fixes and drops. He stares at me, and then quickly smiles again, before being pulled back into the throng.

They are singing a hymn. I hate this hymn. It brings a sour turn to my thoughts. I once said they'd sing this one at my funeral, "God be in my head . . . and in my understanding."

I meet Stephen's college train, because of Grandma's hip. I wait on the three-ridged bench. It smells as if it has been urinated on by a thousand disestablishmentarian teenagers, and their dogs. Using the toilet twelve metres away would presumably compromise their cause.

I re-read his letters.

No, this is not Stephen, my cousin Stephen. Stephen is not stoic, determinedly happy. This stranger describes his girlfriend Miranda, his roommate Joel's conversational inability with girls. The letters are peppered with exclamation marks to tell us where to laugh. We read each one together, Grandma and I, and at the end we raised our heads and looked at each other.

And this handwriting is unfamiliar. I have not seen his handwriting since the childish round cursive which he sent out, scowling, asking if Caroline and Robert would come to Tea With Me for his eleventh birthday party. This adult curvaceous slant expresses pleasure at the birth of Julia's son, joy at the news of Rachel's engagement. That shocks me, although my mother thinks it is nice. It is nice. I do not know this Stephen.

The train has pulled into the station. I am arguing with a tall, close-cropped stranger, who wears glasses, who needs to wear glasses. We cannot decide who should take the bag. We both want to take it, we are too unsure of each other to want to fob this off so that the winner can laugh at the loser. Stephen does not retort, on winning, that I am, after all, a girl. He simply picks up the suitcase and we walk out of the station.

Along the rutted railway track we force parental-style regurgitations. I have been rehearsing this all morning. I hide behind Grandma. "Grandma said to ask you if you liked the new tie." He asks after Julia, Rachel, Robert, my parents, me, Grandma, Julia's baby, school, wedding plans.

"I'm not going back," he says, suddenly.

"You're changing colleges?"

"No. I'm joining the Navy."

I begin to laugh.

"What's so funny about that?"

"You? In the Navy?"

"Yes." He begins to laugh too. He shakes his head. "But I am. I mean it."

I can see Stephen now, struggling to get free.

"Do you want to go paddling?" I ask, tentatively. Will this new girlfriended, bespectacled Stephen want to go paddling?

"Race you," he says.

But he does not start off ahead of me, and does not retort,

on losing, that I am, after all, a girl, he didn't really bother trying. He pants and says he is out of practice. We dangle our feet in the icy, tadpole-infested water and he tells me that Miranda is his roomate Joel's girlfriend and confesses his own conversational inability with girls who don't want to go paddling, or rope climbing, or fishing for newts.

The funeral is over now. Over. The women linger, their huge brimmed hats shadow the open grave. The larger the hat, the longer they linger. There are whispers, no more tears. The gerbil-faced man puts his hand on the shoulder of the blonde girl. "Take your grandmother down to the car, Isobel." There is a clink. Keys.

It is strange. I remember little after that, although I know there is more that I ought to remember. I have the bones of my biography but they have been pecked and polished dry, and there is no meat to put on them. Stephen joined the Navy; he was posted a long way away, India, or South Africa. I remember my own entry to college, Rachel's wedding, the baptism of Julia's second son, my godchild. I remember that I wore white. I remember my brother's graduation, with a feeling of seething embarrassment. I remember the publication of his first book.

I remember a telegram, the telegram. It stood on my grandmother's dresser for three days. Stephen's funeral. I wore a black dress, a little too big. I let my hair down loose, and I cried in all the wrong places.

I have a vague notion of marriage, a daughter, who people insist is a mirror of me.

And I remember something else too. A hospital. Stale food, congealing vomit. Painted light brown to hide the smell of disinfected dirt. The intermittant beep of a green screen monitor.

I am being swallowed and regurgitated. It is light and dark and I am being swallowed and regurgitated, and swallowed and regurgitated. There are cobblestones in the stomach where we can do handstands, but it is too knotted and too slippery in the duodenum. It is noisy down here, too noisy.

"Mum?"

There is pressure on my wrist.

"Mum, it's Isobel."

But I am sliding down into the dark again. I am doing handstands in the stomach and it is far too noisy down here to hear anything except the scream, the running feet, and the rising whine of a green screen which has stopped beeping.

How did I get here? I do not remember. I stand, quietly. I gaze down at my feet. Sneakers? I haven't worn sneakers since I was fourteen. And shorts? Flabby, pea-green shorts. I threw those away the summer after Stephen dropped college.

Stephen. I wish he was here now.

It is late. I should go home. My parents will worry.

I leave the grass. The vicar and the gerbil-faced man talk quietly. I catch, "Your wife Caroline—" They do not look up as I pass them.

I am going home.

This is the top of a hill, and I should see my house from here. I am not wearing glasses, I feel their absence over my nose and behind my ears. I can see every house for miles.

Which way is home?

We used to come up to the top of this hill, me and Stephen and Robert, to see our houses from above, like on a map. Stephen and Grandma lived under a black roof. Me and Robert had a red roof. A red roof. There can't be many houses with red roofs.

The priest and the man part company now. I see the man skid trot down the hill. Wind ruffles the grass, and it is getting dark, but I am warm in my shorts and T-shirt.

My house has a red roof.

I peer into the rapidly accumulating gloom.

Every house has a red roof.

Where is my house? I wish Stephen was here. He was never lost.

"Caroline!"

I spin around.

Barefoot, muddy, waving the green fishing net, Stephen is standing on the edge of the marshy tadpole pond.

"Caroline!" he calls. "Come on!"

I walk towards him. "Where's Robert?"

Stephen shrugs. "He'll be here sooner or later, Caroline. We'll come back for him. Let's go now."

I will have to confess. He will laugh at me. "Stephen, I can't remember the way."

He shakes his head and smiles. "It was like that for me, too, at first." Then, he does something he hasn't done since I was learning to walk. He stretches his hand out to me. "It doesn't matter, Caroline. I can show you."

Hands clasped, we walk together down the muddy stream.

Evan Brown (13) **Henry Cruikshank (14)**

*Memorial

This stone was erected by the people of
Rothiemurchus in affectionate remembrance
of Major General Walter Brook Rice
late Royal Artillery
who was accidentally killed
while skating near
this spot.
26th December 1892
"Till the Lord Comes"

Do you see him there,
Down by the waves that lap no longer?
There he slides above the silent waters,
Skimming the waves that lap no longer.

And did you see him,
As he turned in the centre?
As the sun caught the medals on his chest,
A general's uniform for a soldier,
Ranked in silver,
Proudly polished to display.

And did you see him,
As he headed back to shore,
A twinkle in his blue eye?
And did you ask a question?
Is there good or evil in his heart?
Does he care for those around him,
Did you ask?

And did you see him,
As the water came to life once more?
The torture on his face; pure fear,
The medals on his chest jumping,
Grasping for survival as the water took him,
And swallowed him under.

And did you see them,
The judge and the jury?
Turning to the people of the trees down by the water,
And probing, asking, finding.
"Did you see him?" they asked the trees,
Funnelling the wind across from the mountains,
Down from the windy heights of Cairngorm,
Thrashing the green of the canopy,
And
"Yes, we saw him,"
Is their moan.

But *you* did not see him,
Did you?
Down by the whispering trees and the whispering waves,
You did not see the events,
Of a dead century,
Flow on from the death
That was their cause . . .

All that remains,
Down by the water,
Under the canopy of whispering trees,
Is a standing memorial to the dead soldier,
Thanking for much,
Yet telling little,
Because only the trees saw the death of our soldier,
And they cannot speak,
Of a dead century's deeds.

Francesca Harris (15)

*Rocking Chair

Rhythmic rocking, to and fro,
Easy comfort by the fire,
Wizened hands
On whom the dance of the dolmans has been performed
Folded gently in her lap.
Stroke the cat, smoothing the knitting, adjust the grey skirt,
Then tiny feet set in motion
The rhythmic listing, to and fro.
Love shines through coral
Nestling in time-hollowed caverns
And a smile splits under her upper lip.
To and fro,
Gentle, audible breathing soothes the air.

Then he comes in, and extends a hand of warm, polished bone.
Smiling again, she takes a surprising, firm hold,
And stands out of herself,
He touches her gently
And the dolmans dance backwards
Brown hair flows from the iron-hard bun,
Hands become long and smooth.
A pearly pink smile glows for him
And they walk away, together, forever.

Back in the room. The shell falls forward
Setting the rocking chair in motion,
Swaying gently to the wall.
The cat leaps down for a nocturnal prowl,
The fire glows gently,
And all is peace.

John Finnemore (17)

*The Afterthought

Two graves,
In a village churchyard.
Yew tree black at the end of the day,
Grey stone golden, and white stone grey.

Here Lies:
Thomas Lawrence,
b. 1924, d. 1977. A MAN
For all seasons.
BELOVED
husband of Millie and father of
William,
Andrew,
Julia,
Martin . . .

space.

Millie, seventy, shies away from Inevitable Doom,
But the gravestone sits and waits and knows. The mason
has left room.

Ashes to Dust, Flesh to clay.
Phantom words on the gravestone say:
Also of: Millie, Martin, Andlia, Juliam,
JuliAndreWilliaMartin . . .

The other stone is larger, reaching for the yew,
The light at last is failing, diluted by the dew,
The shadow falls in leaded letters, distorting sad old names.
The man can see they're different. They might be all the same.
actonarmstrongbailycassidycubittdunlopfitzpatrickgillardha
wkerkellymaddermacintoshpikephillipsphillipsrobertstwain
walterswilkiewrightyoung . . .
    No space.
When Tom's name was certain, Millie's name was planned.
The little patch of granite. The little stretch of land.

But even in the massed grief of a
village's tears, they did at least know that
the memorial was full. The mason left no space.
The names sprawl out across the stone, luxurious as
the name of a dead bachelor, filling the space.
The monument was full.

The second list of names was fitted on to the base of the stone.

* * *

The light has gone now.
The tombs are rumoured shapes.
He turns.

His coat shields him from the end of the day.
With a head full of memories, the mason walks away.

Natasha Grunberg (8)

*I Wonder . . .

I wonder what it's like to be in hospital
with nurses all around,
My papa is there all alone,
what is it like to feel unwell?
I miss him very much.
He misses me too –
the best bit is coming home
in a few weeks' time.
I wonder what it's like to be in hospital
with a doctor coming in every second,
with a nurse coming to take your temperature.
Oh! I'd get so dizzy!
I wonder what it's like to be in hospital,
with lots of people visiting you twenty times a day,
with your mother left at home
and your brothers fast asleep.
My papa is there
in hospital
all alone.

I wonder what it's like to be dying
by yourself,
going up to heaven, and people thinking
where have you gone.
I miss you so much now.
I think about you every day.
Your body lies beneath the earth
old and weary.
I miss playing with you,
I miss going over to sleep with you,
I miss touching you,
I miss kissing you.
Do you see me up there?
Do you hear me?
I hear you
but I can't see you.
Why did you have to leave me?
I miss you so much
I do wonder what it's like to be dying, don't you?

Rob McColl (16)

Hovercraft

The hovercraft is packed with the skins
bones, flesh and brains of the businessmen;
(men who go about their business).

First class, second class, compartments,
(carriages, classifications clarify with no
need or room for confusion . . .
though in secret, confusion abounds).

The click clock tick tocks, rhythm in the
crisp air, champagne, claret plops in clear and
splendid globular slops,
(sprinkling as raindrops).

The hostess flushed and sliding over
plush blue carpet, like the hostess (smooth and soft),
among the men she comes and goes,

That she's there, they are aware, as the wine
she simply flows, her glistening enamel smile shines,
but hides the fillings, dark behind (and
elsewhere her holes are
bare).

The hovercraft (craft that hovers above the raging seas).
Froth and bubble, foam and filth, flung with fiery storm
whipped force in waves, on windows, boom and pound
(but inside it makes no sound).

Just silent splash against the panes,
simply a storm, the sea, they sigh (the muted crash
of tide and toiling tempest tossed on glass is lost in the
buzz of the engine).

The wind it roars, the seas they shake, the
champagne pours (and the men they unfold
the daily newspaper, a trifle bored).
Terror, tragedy, death and war (the gale
is howling at the doors) reported on the printed page
(it's all so far away, of course it's just another day
in the newspaper).

Greed and murder ("More champagne, Sir?")
Papers are folded, crinkle clean, with pity and a general sigh,
(the hostess glides just slow enough for eyes and minds to
think about, and then reject, the pinching of an inch
of thigh).

Then thoughts, they fly ahead instead, while the
definitive, clinical clock ticks on, like a
judder in the rudder that steers the brain
anticipation of the next second, and refrain from
the now, stationed like silence, dormant and
dead in the head, itself in thought of the oncoming port
when the journey will begin for real, (until then
we'll pass the time with some news and some wine,
go about our business and we'll all feel fine).

In the craft that hovers, the clock is still ticking
But the captain is ailing and the hostess is wailing,
Funeral-grey are the storms through the day,
(Time is an iceberg and the Hover-Titanic is sailing its way,
away, far away.
The Titanic is sailing our way).

John Furneaux (10)

Handyman

The minute, pink, fat hands of a baby just born
Feeling the new experience.
So many things to learn in so little time.
I start to travel on hands and knees.
Feeling new rooms and places to explore,
More and more tastes,
Things making noises, things not to do,
My mind's in a muddle, everything's new.
But now I'm remembering and starting to understand,
The adult world.
My life rushes by, nursery, primary and junior gone in
a flash.
I now, pen in hand, am using my new-found memory.
Choosing my studies and the stress of exams clutter my
mind.
Making money, graphs of profits, businesses closing down.
Recession killing off shops like plague kills people.
My hands move frantically over a keyboard.
My eyes watch over figures.
Making machines do this and that, a sense of power.
Riches, fame were my target but even my hands can't grab
that much.
The pressure slowly declines as do my knuckles.
My young, bouncy, fat skin is bunching up in wrinkles.
I sit down in my armchair and think about what's past.
Nothing can get it back, not even two hands.
My hands, they served me well.
Brain stops thinking, limbs seize up, skin dies away.
From pink, fat skin to a rotting skeleton: my life.

Barney Jeffries (15)

**Best Before

Past my expiry date
I was taken off the shelf
to be judged.
Weighed in the balance
by austere shop assistants.

Awaiting the verdict
of throw-away-guilty
or sell-at-a-knocked-down-price-guilty
I was intrigued to see
somewhere behind the groceries
a sign reading "Redemption
this way."

So I made my excuses
and ran off,
on after-Best-Before legs
till I came to the redemption department.

"Eternal life in paradise, please,"
said I to the lady behind the counter.
"Ninety-nine ninety-nine,"
she said, "Plus travel."

The price being far too dear,
I trotted off to the bargain rail
where I booked
a cut-price week in an attractive little bedsit
somewhere in the north of Hell.

A HEART THAT THUMPS

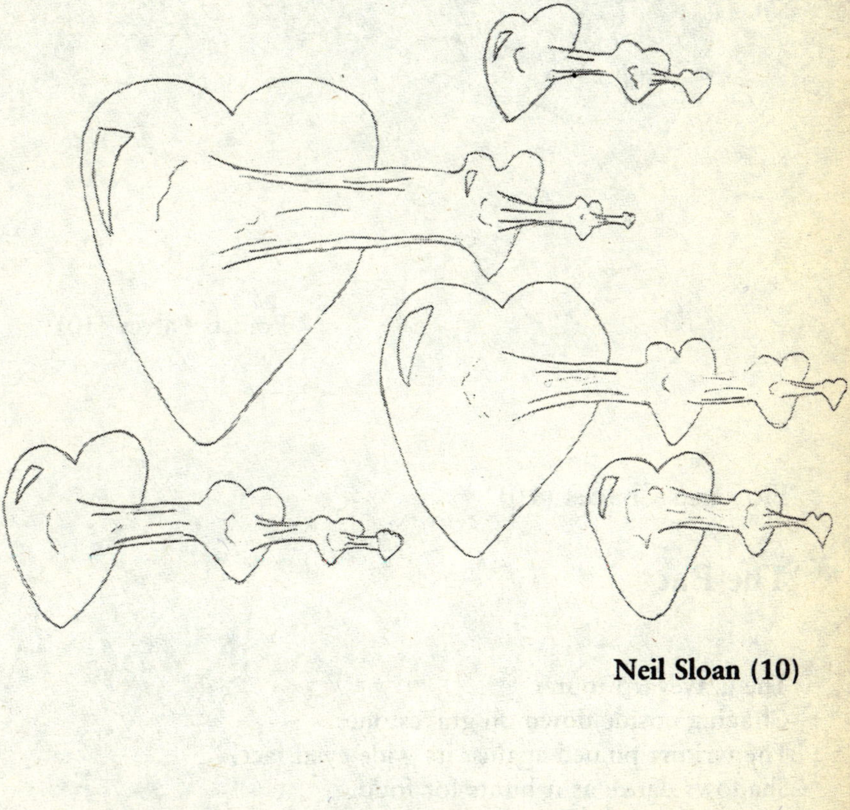

Neil Sloan (10)

Francis Falvey (10)

Florence Chaces (10)

The Bat

The graveyard tourer,
Clinging upside-down on gravestones.
The writing pinned against its wide-eyed face.
Shadows dance as it hunts for food.
Big ears hunting for every sound,
In the twilight zone as the moon emerges.
But as dawn breaks,
This delicate defenceless creature
Takes off his waxed cape and goes to sleep.

Ellen Coffey (6)

The Monster

Under the stairs
amongst old wellington boots,
pillows and blankets
a monster lives.
When I go upstairs
I hear creaking.
It creeps out for a drink,
and I feed it carrots.

Laura Joanne Williams (14)

Danny Manning (11)

*A Night in the Namibian Bush

I was sitting on a small camp stool, looking into the glowing fire, the only source of light. I was holding a mug of thick hot soup in my freezing hands. The occasional cackle of a hyena or roar of a lion broke the silence from time to time, but otherwise it was silent. I felt like we were the last people on earth. There was probably no other living human being within at least fifty miles radius.

"This is the BBC World Service. Here is the news read by . . ."

Everyone looked round at the cheerful words coming from my dad's small transistor radio on the bonnet of the car.

My dad was collecting firewood in a clump of undergrowth about thirty metres from us. You couldn't see him in the dark, you could only hear him rustling in the bushes.

"Dad, come back!"

I was scared something was going to happen to him. I had already seen one dead man that afternoon. And I had overheard my mum telling him to watch out for snakes, especially in the dark. Cobras are night hunters.

Peter came back dragging an enormous log.

"This should last us the night."

"You're gonna keep the fire going all night?" said my sister Emily.

"It's just a bit safer. It'll keep the animals at a good distance."

I knew what he meant.

I got up from the stool without saying anything. I took my shoes off and crawled into the tent. I didn't bother changing into my pyjamas or brushing my teeth. I felt too scared to stay awake.

Emily came in too and lay down. Peter popped his head in and said, "Good night." I lay there in my sleeping bag listening for what seemed like hours. Suddenly my heart jumped. An enormous snort came from just behind the tent. I held my breath. Whatever it was kept on snorting. I wished I was in the same tent as my parents.

Then I heard my parents speaking.

"What's that?" Mum whispered loudly.

"I don't know," said Dad. "It could be a hippo. They come a long way to graze."

I relaxed. But I wouldn't have if I knew then what I know now, which is that hippos, even though they are vegetarians, are responsible for more human deaths than any other animal in Africa. They chop you in half with their giant jaws.

Next morning I woke up early and unzipped the front of the tent. My dad was making coffee on the still glowing fire.

"Come and see this," he said, and led me to a spot about ten metres from our two tents. There, in amongst the elephant footprints which we had got used to seeing, crossing over our own dusty car tracks from the night before, were some more fresh footprints, large and padded and a bit like a cat's.

"That was a lion!" said my dad.

Nisha Doshi (7)

*An Indian Eclipse

The burning-hot, glimmering sun shines down on fields of brown grass and dying plants. Thirsty, weary peasants trudge along the dry, dusty dirt-road to collect water from the village pump. Starving bullocks, with long, floppy ears and small, curved horns, tramp along in front of the peasants. The overhead sun casts short, sharp shadows on the ground. The sun is a huge ball, burning in the azure sky.

In the village, a chilli seller sits in the scorching sun, wearing a chilli-coloured turban. The vegetable stall keeper shouts across the street, "Buy my vegetables! My tasty, fresh vegetables!" There are purply-black aubergines, juicy pink pomegranates and strong, sweet-smelling herbs, all set out neatly in the cool shade. The heat from the blazing sun makes babies cry and dogs bark. A one-armed beggar sits cross-legged, under the shade of a tree, pleading for scraps of food. The sun is still a huge, fiery ball burning in the azure sky.

Suddenly, the sky becomes darker and darker, as if a giant hand has covered the sun. There is not a cloud to be seen. Everyone starts to panic. Children are screaming with fright. Mothers run around, calling their names and dragging them home. Some old women pray to the gods to keep them safe. The chilli seller quickly packs away his chillies and salt, and hurries off to find shelter. The vegetable seller shouts for help and prays that the gods will keep his vegetables safe. Men working in the fields, drop their tools and run to the village, terrified.

After a few minutes, everything is pitch black! The village is silent. Everyone waits for something dreadful to happen.

Nothing happens.

After a short while, the sky gradually becomes lighter. The sun begins to shine again. Everyone is relieved, the darkness has passed over. Nothing dreadful happened. Slowly, everything goes back to normal. The men go back to the fields, the children come out to play again, and the stall keepers start selling chillies and vegetables again. The sun is a huge, fiery, scorching ball, burning in the azure sky.

Eimear O'Brien (8)

Being Afraid

Being afraid is
a dry mouth
a heart that thumps
and tears
on the long, long journey to the operating theatre.

Feeling better is
a Derry strip in
one hand
and Mummy's hand in the other.

Robert Hill (10)

*The Ghostly Boots

At night
All the foot bones
In the graveyard
Grow skin
And rise
Hunters hunt them down
The feet use a
Shield Suddenly the
Wooden wall collapses
The feet scatter everywhere
But are captured by the
Hunters – they are shot at
But they don't die,
No one knows why and
No one knows whose
Ghostly boots they are.

Ann Berry (12)

*Scissors

Mother is cutting material, she is going to make a dress.
Mother sees scissors, I don't.

I see a mother holding her child, caressing her baby in
her arms.
She rocks him gently to and fro,
Feeling nothing but love for the child she has born.

Mother sees scissors, I don't.

I see Siamese twins, pulling and pushing, desiring liberty –
Wanting to escape from the tight bond that holds them
so tightly
That they cannot get free.

Mother is cutting material, she is going to make a dress.
Mother sees scissors, I don't.

Ben Dryer (16)

Barney Jeffries (15)

**Under-river

A song, loosely inspired by Mervyn Peake's "Titus Alone"

Underneath the river
With one hand on my life,
I met a failed author
Who clutched a kitchen knife
He slept upon his books
As they yellowed with the years
He told me he wrote tragedy
But wasn't keen on tears
"The one and only problem
Is that no one here can read"
We had quite a conversation
And these words stayed with me:
Underneath the river
We have everything and nothing
We are happy, we are sad
We are slaves and we are free
And we do not know the meaning
Of the words you keep repeating
Like "war", "ambition", "win"
And "jealousy".

Underneath the river
Thinking thoughts of suicide
I met an ageing man who swore
He'd never been outside
He said he'd heard the stories
About trees and sky and rain
But considered them inventions
Of some over-active brain
He'd been born in Under-river
And there he'd soon be dead
And he'd never lived elsewhere
And this is what he said:
    Underneath the river
    We have everything and nothing
    We are happy, we are sad
    We are slaves and we are free
    And we do not know the meaning
    Of the words you keep repeating
    Like "war", "ambition", "win"
    And "jealousy".

An assassin in a waistcoat
A rich man faint from thirst
A bishop in a pulpit
Who tells us that we're cursed
A twenty-six stone woman
With a baby at her breast
And a long retired pirate
Sleeping on his treasure chest
Underneath the river
Faces float my way
And somewhere in the silence
I think I hear them say:
  Underneath the river
  We have everything and nothing
  We are happy, we are sad
  We are slaves and we are free
  And we do not know the meaning
  Of the words you keep repeating
  Like "war", "ambition", "win"
  And "jealousy".

And the river roaring overhead
Will soon leave all these strangers dead
As it makes its endless journey
To the sea
No hymns from tower and steeple
For these forgotten people
Their names engraved on tombstones
That no one ever reads.

Sally Gillo (10)

*Guilt in the Wood

I want to lie down and become the wood,
But I don't want to get stung by nettles.
Even though the nettles make me angry
I don't want to let down the wood.
Even though the trees are rotting
They are still far more beautiful than you.
I am wearing rubber in the wood:
That's why the stinging nettles lean forward to sting me.
I have broken the promise I made to the trees.
I feel scared.
The nettles are growing taller
And making me feel small.
My eyes circle around the wood.
Everything is against me.
I feel guilty because I am wearing rubber boots.
I feel like taking them off
And stinging and staining my feet.

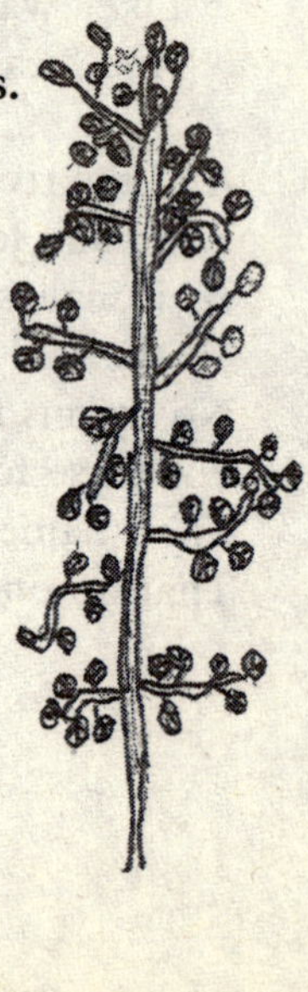

Gary Sergeant (11)

LITTER-FILLED WASTELANDS, OIL-FILLED LAKES

Freya Elliot (11)

Emma Charlton (12)

Whose Fault Is It?

Who killed the trees?
"I," said the saw,
"They felt my jagged jaw,
I killed the trees."

Who turned you on?
"I," said the man,
"The law says I can,
I turned it on."

Who saw them die?
"I," said the breeze,
"As they fell to their knees,
I saw them die."

Who shall suffer?
"I," said the squirrel, "I and my friend,
For our little world has come to an end,
We shall suffer."

Who else shall suffer?
"I," said the chief of a tribe in despair,
"You trample our homes and you don't even care,
We shall suffer."

Who gets the profit?
"I," said the boss with a satisfied smile,
"You gave me an inch and I chopped down a mile,
I get the profit."

Who decides what happens when the trees are cut down?
"I," said the rich millionaire owner, "They're felled every day,
They're made into paper, written on, and then thrown away,
I decide what happens."

Who decides what happens to the land?
"I," said the rich millionaire, "By then it's not nice,
So who cares, no big deal, it's not used twice,
I decide what happens to the land."

Whose fault is it?
"It is yours, it is mine, we must all take the blame,
We cut down the trees and don't plant them again,
It is our fault."

Jemma Gray (11)

*O, Badger!

O, badger this used to be your home,
In fields of bluebells,
Creeping out from tree-roots
Shuffling through moonlight.

Then diggers arrived
That dig more fiercely than you,
Killing your friends,
Ruining your dwelling.

Now we see you
Padding up hard concrete paths,
Startled by your loss.

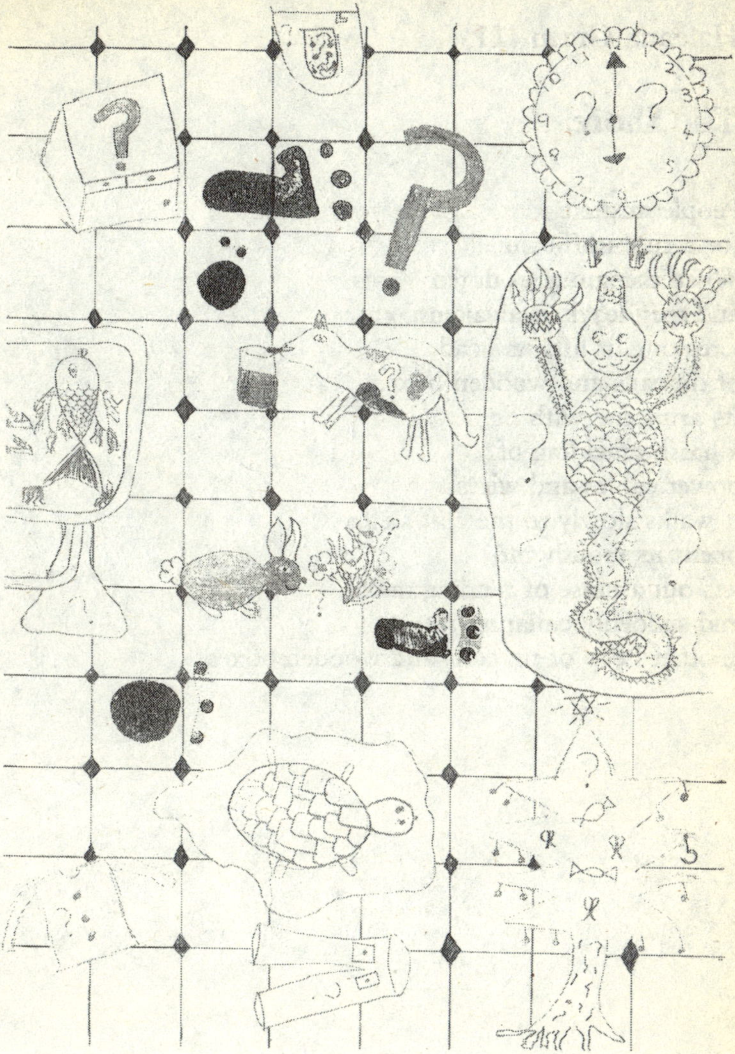

Sally Brown (10)

Haleana Green (11)

The Shore

People mistake it
for a rubbish heap.
When the sun goes down
and they leave, it awakens.
Creaking, it lifts its head
of tin cans and wooden boxes.
Its arms rise with
a harsh crackling of
power cables and wires.
It walks slowly to the cliff's edge,
opens its mouth and
lets out a noise of rending metal,
and suddenly collapses into
another heap of tin cans and wooden boxes.

Thomas Newdick (14)

Freight Yard

The City of Manchester
Hauling blackened trucks
Shadowed by giant, grey, cooling towers
Puffing oily dark smudges into the cloudless blue sky.
The glossy grey train momentarily quickens
Before plunging into the darkness of an under-hill tunnel.

The William Shakespeare
Struggles through its cluttered freight yard,
Drags behind its mixed load of clanking trucks
Piled wih rusting rails, rotten planking, broken crates.
The train groans before clattering to a standstill.

The Lord Nelson,
In tattered scratched battle paint
His scruffy vans marching behind.
Thick, black, choking smoke seeps from vents,
As he hauls box waggons past the platform,
Filled with McVitie's biscuits, Sheerness Steel, Wotsits,
Engine parts, Pot Noodles.

The Fife and Forfar Yeomanry
Drags battered cement-filled trucks
Under a steel spider's web of overhead cables
Past shining concrete and glass office blocks,
Through litter-filled wastelands, oil-stained lakes
And rusty car skeletons, awaiting their
Inevitable fate in the breaker's yard.

Kathryn Williams (11)

Sophie Carter-Ingram (11)

Going, Going, Gone

That will be Earth,
Lot one million, four hundred thousand, five hundred and forty nine.
Galactic space auction,
Fifth of August two thousand one hundred and twenty one A.D.
We are here today to decide who will now own it
As the oldest known owner
Has tired of its mayhem and destruction.

It is an inhabited planet,
If you can call its savage, greedy, destructive people inhabitants.
They exist in crowded, polluted cities
for only three per cent of empty, unaffected space
Is left.
What animals remain
Are cowering, frightened,
On the lookout all the time.

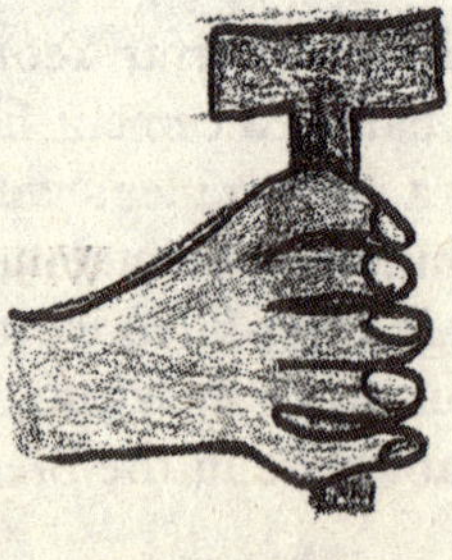

Kathryn Williams (11)

I see a hand going up,
How much am I bid?
One pound?
Any advance on a pound?
Come come, this Earth has great potential,
No more bids?
No?
Well it's going
Going,
Gone.
Sold to the man in the corner
With the red horns.

Katie Hern (10)

Kathryn Williams (11)

Peter Mitchell (11)

The Raft

Slowly, almost imperceptibly,
rolling out slow tragedy after slow tragedy,
the sluggish raft of time
drifts, drifts, drifts
towards the harbour bar
the point of no return
where the smooth river,
blackening as it passes
through the grey metropolis
meets the heavy, heaving, blacker sea.

The raft is perfectly balanced –
it needs to be,
for it carries on its coarse, green wood
the massive weight of civilizations,
a thousand million billion atoms
of a whole body
that sways the raft,
making the water lop over the binding-ropes,
rotting them.

More, who before swam in the deathly cold water
that they themselves created,
cling on, and board.
They feel safe,
but the raft unsteadies under their added weight.

The wind from the surging ocean
breathes the cold of death
into their freezing limbs.
They stare at each other
then abruptly look away,
ashamed at the thought
passing through their minds –
that once the raft is in the open sea
the stronger will have to drown
or eat
the weaker.
They know it will happen.

The raft nears the harbour bar,
now more must be picked up
their anguished cries soothed,
their freezing bodies warmed.
But they unsettle the raft further –
their cold cannot be cured:
already the chill ocean winds blow stronger,
the raft draws nearer to the bar.

The raft has a paddle but
O, irony of ironies!
the riders do not see it,
though they are well aware of its presence.
One, maybe two, reach out and grope for it
but they only push their hands
as far as the very tip,
from which the paddle cannot be lifted
for use.
The others only live for the present.
They pick up swimmers
do not glance at the approaching swell,
but concentrate on themselves instead.

Only one out of thirty billion rafters is sane.

This is a raft of fools.

Evan Brown (13)

*Islands in the Desert

The sky drifts past in paint-stroke puffs of red and orange. In the distance, a deep star-studded indigo over the sky-scrapered horizon, where large buildings tumble up into the sky. Here and there, pinprick neon lights in the desert. Tyres hum softly on the black road which leads straight into the distance, to the city, a neon island of day-in-night. The speedometer needle hovers up and down. Curiosity grows about what lies at the end of the silk-smooth highway with its cars which fly silently along, red lights glimmering nearer or drawing further away. Then, the interstate sign whips past: "Welcome to Las Vegas."

You pass through a dazzling maze of shops, hotels and casinos. Flashing signs promote different commodities and services. People by night at the wheel; quicksilver flashes; faces suggesting stories, which gust away as car horns wail restlessly.

The breeze of quiet motors dwindles as you pass swiftly through the city, mile after mile, street after street, light after light. And then you leave the hubbub, the strange freedom of nightlife, and you are free beneath the sky. The highway is quiet as you head, once again, into the desert.

Hour after hour, your headlights pick out pale roadside sagebrush, spiky ocotillos and prickly pears, until a light approaches with almost imperceptible slowness to spell out, FOOD.

Mike's Eating Place is nowhere in particular, but life spills out of its lighted windows. Trucks stand silently in the sand, or pull up with noisy engines shattering the night until the shiny vertical exhausts shudder into silence.

Plain, tiled floor, and plain, cold brick walls bearing the

garish propaganda of the distant city. Tables and benches with high, imitation-leather backs. A few men line a bar in one corner, sipping black coffee and eating chunks of pie.

A plain woman puts colas, burgers and tacos down on the plain tables. She does not say anything. She just does it. Then she goes. But just the way she does it, the plain, everyday, easygoing routine is something special. Something ordinary, but something strange and thrilling. Just the way her hair is done. Plain brown, casual curls. Her face is open, glasses wide, lips unpainted. Red T-shirt and apron. The way she carries three dishes on the same hand, swaggering confidently past the male diners.

It is just a place where people come and eat, pay and leave. Sitting at the tables, dangling their feet to the plain, tiled floor, breathing the air, full of beef and fries. She swaggers towards your table, paper in hand.

"How far to San Diego, Miss? About three hours?"

She smirks:

"Well, I'd get there one whole lot sooner'n that!"

There is something enthralling in her brief, violent reply; the freedom of her words, as she heads away and you leave the restaurant in its insignificant place by the edge of the great desert highway.

Just fifteen miles south of San Diego on Interstate Five, the United States comes to an end. Here, in this medley of turnstiles and bureaucracy, passports and papers, legality and illegality, Mexico begins.

You leave your car in the car-park and stroll through a creaking pedestrian gate into Tijuana. Pause and look behind you, but already you have been digested by swarms of black, brown and white people. The air is different, saturated, foreign. It carries the scent of Mexican food, perfume, dirt and poverty.

A concrete bridge takes you over the stink of effluent to

the diseased ruins of Mexico. The last signs for the US border seem to appeal to you not to descend past the graffiti-scrawled walls into the heaving crowd below. Gone are the big shops, the department stores. Instead, seedy cafés in back alleys where tourists with cameras and binoculars, straw hats and boxer shorts eat and drink, while from all sides they are assailed by children as young as two or three, holding trays with homemade pouches, necklaces and other trivia.

You make way for Indian women with babies wrapped in rags. American children are told by their parents to ignore the salesmen and beggars, and stick close, while all the time the sidewalks are lined with people, lying, crouching and sitting; everyone selling the same things as everyone else.

Better-off tradesmen hawk cheap jewellery which dangles from their arms.

"Hey, *amigo*!" You wanna buya necklace for de wife?" People in rag uniforms yell "Taxi!" to the passing Americans, and sunglassed faces turn away.

You stop at a sidewalk café, where American radio plays loudly. A waiter approaches, his left arm in a sling of dirty bandages, takes your order and disappears. Everything on sale here is American. American cigarettes, American soft-drinks, and only the straw hats which line ramshackle shelves have MADE IN MEXICO stamped in ink under the rims.

And after you finish, pay the chit and tip the waiter, you move on, past the clapped out red buses with "MEXI-COACH – The Easy Way to See Mexico" painted on them in large black letters, and on, down a side street, where tourists do not go as a rule, and you stop by a shop, where little children crowd round a television, watching *Tom and Jerry* from the 1960s. You reflect on what you have seen, and conclude that the whole country feasts on the flotsam of American society.

And then with tired feet, and lots to think about, you

return to San Diego and the United States, needing at most a stamp in a passport – while some wade through rivers of sewage, climb barbed fences and run the gauntlet of Interstate traffic to reach their goal. Back at your hotel, you eat fast food for supper, and settle down in front of the television, to watch *Tom and Jerry*, from the 1960s.

Sarah Barrow (12)

Famine

Somewhere in the desert,
just somewhere in the world
a small boy has stopped

Somewhere in the distance
a large vulture waits
for a lost child
of the human race

Somewhere in the world
below the lowest thought
beneath the burning sun
a life is done

Somewhere in the world
where we've never been
starving children have no food
they die every second
but we only watch
like the hungry bird.

A LANDSCAPE IN GOD'S MOUTH

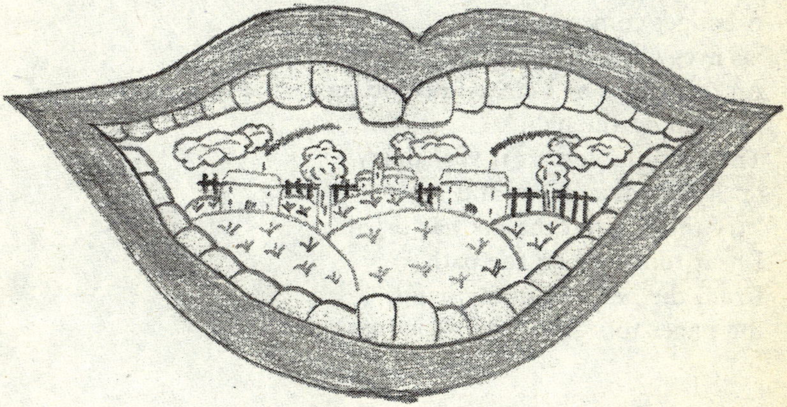

Melissa Southerland (12)

Ellen Coffey (6)

The Garden

It is night-time.
I climb over the gate tied up with string,
I see wild flowers . . .
There are foxgloves,
and poppies amongst daisies and roses.
A badger comes out,
his eyes glitter as he looks at me.
An owl hoots as I creep into the shed,
I switch on the light.
There is a table that is very dusty,
on it lies some paper and a pen.
I try the pen but the ink has dried.
I hear footsteps on the path.
I run, the pen still in my hand,
the paper too.

Katherine Brown (7)

The Seed

Stretching grey roots,
The tree in a case.
There's silver dew on the tip.
It's ready to emerge.
The next day it appeared.
Tall was the shoot and the small stem too.
But the seed has split its pyjamas
And shed its plant.

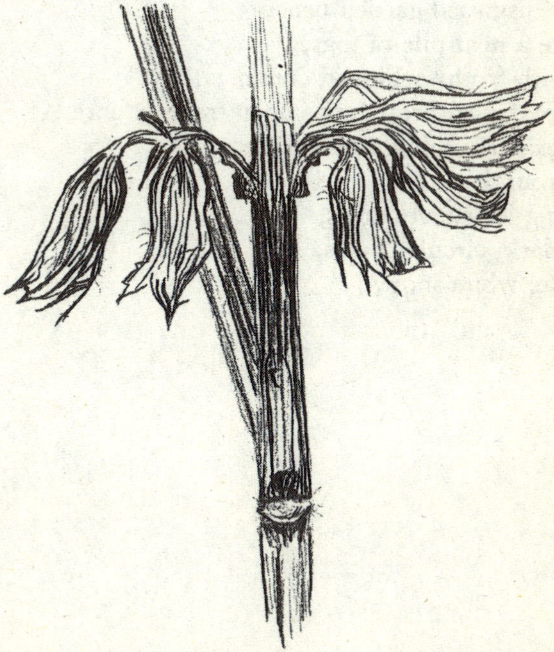

Rowena Scanlon (15)

Nisha Doshi (7)

*Patterns in the Snow

The dark lines of car tyres
Criss-cross paper white roads,
Like the intricate patterns
Of a Celtic manuscript.
Winding trails of oval footprints
In pairs reveal the charcoal-grey pavement,
Hidden beneath a milky-white carpet.
The edges of snow-covered roof tiles
Ripple gently, like wages on a frozen white sea.
The snow-disguised garden bench
Stands like a neat pile of logs,
Topped with frothy whipped cream.
Snowflakes dance through the open trellis squares,
Like fairies performing an ice ballet.
And all around,
The melting ice slowly drips,
Forming dark, circular holes,
In the pure, white snow.

Rebecca Walsh (15)

Rock Calls for Rain

rock calls for rain
and warm beneath
the roots again
and curls again
that hold returns
inhales the sky
to fill and light
the sleepless trees
to light above
the spinning hill
to cloak the ground
and hide the rock
in pouring cries
to pounding air
and falling high
inside the storm
and warm inside
and leaves above
and hide beneath
the grass again

Andrew Frank (8)

Christmas Snow

I woke up. Snow at last!
White, glittering snow.
Tractor marks spoil the smoothness,
Frost sparkles on the tips of the grass.

I run out with my sister,
And pull her on our bright blue sledge.
Birds swoop through the air,
And sad sheep try to graze.

Dad pushes the snow from the door
With his tractor.
Mum is lighting the fire and dusting.
And the cats are near the fire fast asleep.

Laura Lynch (7)

Clouds

Roses as white as snow
Budding and bursting
Petals float from blooms
Flying and fluttering in the blue
Like lilies on a pond
In a sky garden.

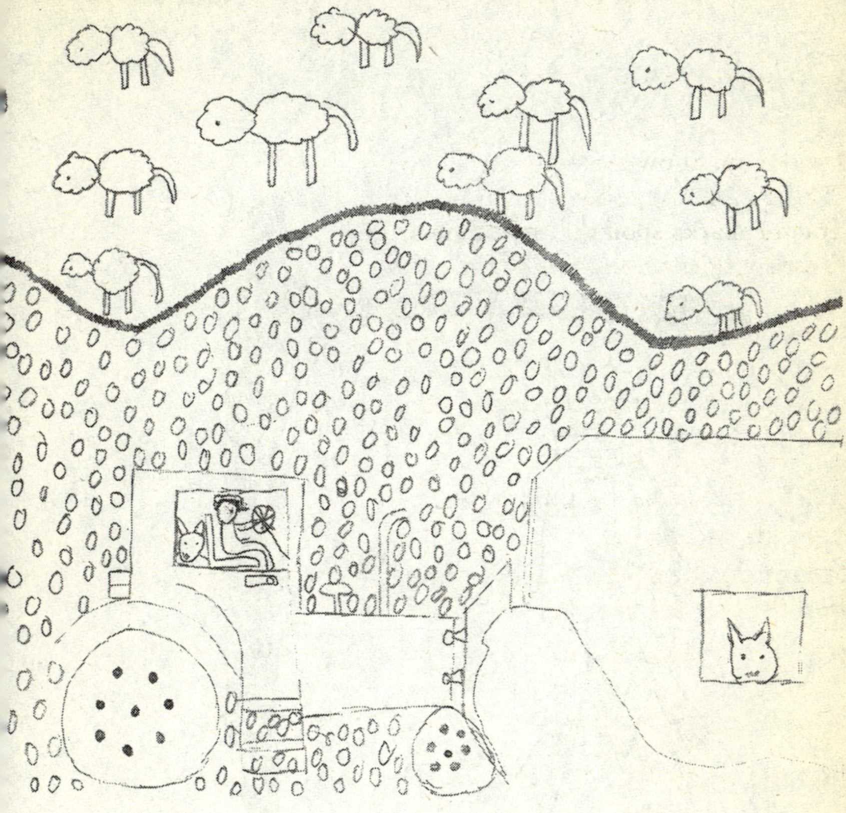

Andrew Frank (9)

Elizabeth Holden (8)

Elizabeth Holden (8)

*Snow Woman

A winter's night,
And in the cold outside,
A snow woman forms.

Her icy fingers touch,
Her split snake-tongue flickers,
Her evil eyes stare.

Her nails strike down trees,
Her eyes still, and mad.
Night creatures flee.

She grins,
Her laughter echoing.

As a splinter of light
Snatches at her gown
Her feet vanish,
Her ankles, knees and thighs,
Her cackles silenced.

She grabs the empty air,
Her head sliding.
Her hand reaches one last time,
But she is gone.

Helena Stebbug (7)

Molly Willcocks (7)

*Out on the Moors

When I went
Out on the moors
I wore my cloak
I wore boots.

It was very windy
Out on the moors
I wrapped my cloak tight
And pushed through the air.

I saw a snake slither by
Out on the moors.
I felt rain on my cheek.

I could hear chirping of birds
Out on the moors,
I could feel bracken brushing on my legs.

There were sheep
Out on the moors.
There were branches blowing in the air
And there was a swan swimming on the pond.

It was dull
Out on the moors.
There were flies sitting on rocks
The wind blew in my hair.

There was barbed wire
Out on the moors.
I could hear rain on my coat
And snakes were hissing.

There were ducks
Out on the moors.
It was nearly night
That was my day out on the moors.

Jessie Binns (16)

**Festival

A gorge in the ground
We were the river running in the base
Water of tarmac, froth of white car.
I gazed up at the sides, the flanks of grass
on ribs of crags
The rocks, the dales.

A house for sale, a ford, a stile.
A climb. Ingleborough! The mosses, the marshes
The smell of the wild, of the earth.
The freedom of space, we ran like a river
We climbed with the wind.

Bread as soft and springy as turf,
Water as clear as the air.
With a shrill that sent shivers through your blood
A steam train burst like a fountain from the hill,
The noise uncertain, rippled off the lake.
Seen in the distance, steam and smoke
and speed and water
Left with the fading of a thunderstorm.

A stepping-stone climb. The stones
of the summit. We shared our talk and
Our bread with the sheep and the wind.
The view was silent to our wind-numbed ears
Silent and huge.
And safe.

A day or two later; a stroll to a waterfall
The silvery cornets, grey, light and white water.
The quiet power of music, the spellbound pool.
Hardraw Force and the red of the stones
Echoes of trees, faces, brass bands and the beer tent.

We will return soon
'Though the people, the places, the names
may be different,
The air and the space are the same.
All are free.

Patrick Maguire (10)

Peace

Hills in the background
like invisible waterfalls.
The hills run into the sky.
The river runs over the world
a landscape in God's mouth.

TO WALK THE HIGH WIRE

Henry Cruikshank (14)

Nisha Doshi (7)

*The Two Faces of Mount Everest

Magnificent, magical, mighty mountain,
Elegant Queen of the Himalayas.
Chomolungma,
Stairway to the stars.
Your ivory icicles hang from rocks
Like stalactites in diamond caves.
While glorious, gleaming glacial snakes
Glide down the slippery slopes
To the enchanted valleys below.
A peaceful breeze gently blows,
And your pure, glistening, velvety snow
Reflects the bright, frosty sunlight
And the misty grey plateaux,
Like a huge, glossy mirror
High on your sparkling, silver summit.

Merciless, murderous, mighty mountain,
Heartless Queen of the Himalayas.
Your shadowy, gloomy, jagged rocks
Scowl at the cruel, ashen sky.
While an angry gale screams,
Tearing huge chunks of ice
From glaciers,
Which descend your rugged slopes,
Stumbling and falling over loose rocks
And cloud-covered crags.
Whirling spirals of snow are swept up,
And half-cover perilous crevasses,
Waiting like deadly traps to swallow climbers.

And violent avalanches crash down,
Crushing climbers,
Burying them alive,
Before they reach your savage, scolding summit!

Sally Gillo (10)

*Free Life

I stand on top of the world
And watch the foxes dart
In every direction.
My hair brushes against my cheek
And I cry my cry
Out down into the valley.
I feel like a fox watching its cubs,
But instead I am watching
A wood which has gone wild.
My hair turns into brambles,
My arms and legs turn into branches,
My body turns into a trunk,
I turn into a tree.
Then my arms and legs grow reddish fur
And my head suddenly
Has a nose which smells the wild breeze.
I am a tree fox.
I roll in the grass and gaze at the sun.
My eyes sparkle and flash like diamonds.
I twitch my ears and hear
The happiness ring like a bell.

Sophie Beck (12)

Carl Weclawek (13)

*Number Five's Alive!

The following is a true account of the birth of my cat, Orson's, first litter of kittens, who are now approximately twelve weeks old.

It was the early hours of a Saturday morning on the 11th August 1993. My father had agreed that, should Orson give birth that night, then I would be allowed to stay up to watch over her. It was a truly wonderful experience, and one that I wouldn't have missed for anything!

The cat went to her nest at about 1.37 a.m. – Orson finally began to give birth to her kittens. I watched her stomach moving around significantly, and assumed that her contractions had started. At 1.40 a.m. the water sac appeared about half-way out and the exact birth time was at 1.45 a.m. and ten seconds.

I saw Orson's sharp teeth appear as she bit at the sac. The first kitten was released! It was a magical moment for me! She licked it straight away all over. It was wet, and looked like a little hamster, without any ears. It was so *tiny*! I was still waiting to see its exact markings. Orson was continually making very small, kitten-like sounds, or very small miaows. She looked up at me with her huge green eyes from time to time – I wished that I could have helped her, but she purred at me, and that made me feel really good.

I heard what sounded like a small sneeze, or maybe it was my imagination. I sat there wondering about nature, and how many creatures are able to survive, whatever the conditions.

At 1.58 a.m. there appeared large signs of contractions. Her stomach was really contorting, I felt like I wanted to do something but I didn't want to disturb Orson at her ministrations. Yet again, large waves of contractions seemed to shake her whole body. At 1.59 a.m. Orson was still making little squeaking noises, suddenly she twisted herself over and lay on her back, with all four legs in the air. I had to smile to myself – she did look funny!

At 2.01 a.m. I managed to have a good look at the first kitten. It was black, like Orson, who is sleek black all over, and one quarter Persian, but this little cat's nose looked very pink, and it had two white front paws which looked just like a pair of socks. It was so cute and tiny. It made straight for a nipple, which was its first drink. It was as though it did it automatically. Amazing!

The second kitten appeared to meet the human world at 2.04 a.m. It seemed to just pop out. I noticed that this one had a small, white front to its face. What a surprise! Dad must have been, perhaps, black and white? I wondered too myself – how many more to go? Number Two kitten seemed like a bit of a moaner to me, because he hadn't stopped screaming yet! It seemed to get irritated at being licked, I thought he was anxious to get to the bar! I just had another good look at it, and he or she seemed to have two white paws, with a patch of white from his nose down to his chin. He reminded me of Sylvester, the cat who stars in cartoons with Tweety-Pie. Orson had not stopped licking Sylvester (as I now called him), the moaner, who was *still* moaning! The time was now 2.12 a.m.

I noticed Sylvester also seemed to have a big, white patch on his back right leg. Stupid little cat, he had just stuck his nose into Orson's left ear, perhaps he was searching for a nipple? I thought to myself that this little one would be a character, for sure. Both kittens looked so small and thin.

The time was now 2.18 a.m., and, yes, you've guessed it, Sylvester was still moaning, and Orson was still licking it (probably to shut it up!). Apart from the moaning, the house was otherwise very quiet indeed. Everybody else was in bed, and I looked forward to informing my brother and my foster-sister of the graphic details.

At 2.20 a.m. Number One lost Orson's nipple, and started to moan, but Number Two finally found a nipple – at last! I looked closely at Number One, and I found that he may have had a little patch of white on his chin, although I couldn't quite see clearly.

It was 2.25 a.m. and Orson was starting to eat the umbilical cord, which looked just like a piece of gossamer or coloured string, and the placenta, which looked just like a piece of liver. (YUK!) However, she still looked larger to me, and that suggested that, perhaps, there were more babies to come. Sure enough, she began more contractions. I can't tell you how wonderful this was to watch. This time, as Number Three was born, Orson didn't seem to be disturbed in the slightest. This made me calm down a bit, too. I felt so lucky being able to keep her company!

2.30 a.m. and Orson was on her back again, legs in the air, and you could see the ripples of contractions going up and down her stomach. I also noticed that there was still a great deal of licking going on all of the time. Poor Orson was beginning to look a little tired now.

Well, it was now 2.35 a.m. and everything was silent for just a few seconds. Orson's nest seemed to be ripped and stained with blood, perhaps not from Orson, but from the placenta. I'm not really very well up on these things. I'll have to ask my auntie. (She's a midwife.)

Number Three arrived at 2.38 a.m. exactly, as I checked with the kitchen clock. This one appeared to be completely black, apart from a little touch of white on its tail. It hadn't moaned as much as Number Two, but again it is looking very hard for a nipple. It kept missing; I had to chuckle to myself! It started off in the right direction, but when it got anywhere near, it started going off in the opposite direction.

The last new born (how many more, I asked myself!) had sneezed twice, put its mouth around a nipple, and then, yes, moaned and lost it, and started the same process all over again!

Believe it or not, it was now 2.44 a.m. and Orson seemed to be having a few more contractions. I saw the whole birth this time! It arrived in a bag, which looked as though it was plastic. This one had a white chin, and the very first thing it did was to make a sucking motion, as if it were sucking a nipple. Orson kicked off the "plastic bag", and it came to life! Absolutely fabulous feeling for me! This one also looked as though it may have had two white feet on its back paws, whereas the last one's white bits only went up to its knees!

I began to feel very sleepy now, and I hoped that I would be able to stay awake. I felt that I had to, for Orson's sake.

Orson's fur coat was now very wet. I felt so sorry for her, and I wished that it could be all over for her in a way, but with four kittens to lick, she hardly had time to lick herself.

With about six nipples to choose from, so far, I noticed that only three kittens at any one time seemed to be feeding. I suppose that they all wanted the one that the other one had. Sheer greed – even at that age!

Oh no! Orson began to show more contractions. I hoped for her sake that they were false, but – oh no! Another one, as Number Five arrived. Poor Orson, she had her work cut out to feed this brat pack!

I was now looking at Number Five quite closely. It was all black in colour, but something made me feel that this one was not well. I was not quite sure why. It seemed to be taking a lot longer to recover from its birth, and was definitely much smaller than the others, although it did miaow to Orson. It still had not moved though. I picked it up very gently, and moved it a little. It didn't even cover the size of the palm of my hand. It did however move by itself. Although, if I guessed right, then I thought that Number Five had the least chance of survival. I tried for ages to hold it up to a nipple, but it just refused to grab it at all, even when its lips were stuck to it. Perhaps it needed some stimulation that I didn't know about. I began to feel very nervous about this.

It was now 3.30 a.m. and I was till attempting to help Number Five, poor little thing. I had been trying for fifteen minutes. It still hadn't taken a nipple yet, but strangely pushed the others away from the nipple by using sheer strength of instinct. I hoped that it would get the idea soon. I was also concerned about its breathing. The whole of its back arched with every breath that it took. Poor old Number Five.

At 3.44 a.m. yet another birth took place. This one was a real little wriggler. I took the others away from Orson for a few minutes to allow her time to cope with Number Six. This one too, as far as I could see was all black. Yes, I picked it up, and found that it *was* all black. Maybe I was wrong, but this one was long haired – perhaps it was Orson's quarter of Persian coming out.

I was still fearful for Number Five. I didn't know whether to call my father down or not. It was now 3.49 a.m. It wasn't even as strong as Number Six. I was trying to help it to find a nipple again. I tried for ages, despite the detriment of the others, but alas, to no avail. I was sad to admit that I thought it would probably die by the morning, and every breath it took was torture to me as I watched its little back contorting. I was sure that I had read somewhere that if they died anywhere near the birth-place, then the mother would eat the body. I then realized how important it was that I stayed awake. At least it was alive!

It was now 3.53 a.m. There was still no change in Number Five. I decided that Orson would not have any more kittens now. She looked thoroughly worn out, but so peaceful – what a star!

I placed some fresh paper into the box, and then threw away the blood-stained sheets.

I had one final check, a photograph and then off to bed I went. You little beauties! Still no change in Number Five.

"Goodnight and farewell, you lovely little creatures . . ."

Number Five died at 4.40 p.m. the following afternoon.

Elizabeth Holden (8)

Daniel Langford (8)

*The Big Red Engine Rides Again

It was one of those nights when everybody was asleep. I bet the only people awake in the whole town were the milkman and the bakerman. I suppose it was about four o'clock. I was snoring my head off when suddenly: BEEP BEEP BEEP! I sat up in bed trying to figure the noise out. Was it the alarm clock Mum kept by her bed? No, it was louder than that, what could it be? Then I knew it was Dad's fire brigade bleeper. It was bleeping its head off. Someone somewhere needed the fire brigade!

Dad shot out of bed. No time to lose, no time to lose. He got dressed double fast which is hard when you are supposed to be asleep. The bedroom door burst open and Dad came charging down the hall and out the door like a rocket. I could hear his shoes banging as he ran to his car. The door slammed and the engine gave a roar and off he goes – flat out. This is the bit I hate. We have to wait to see if Dad was quick enough this time to get to the engines. I imagine where he is going, what will he be doing!

Dad skids his car as he zooms off. It is very frosty and the car windows won't clear. His breath is freezing on the glass so he has to stick his head out of the window to see where he is going. The cold wind makes his eyes water. He can't go as fast as he wants because if he should crash he will never get there. As he goes down the hill to the fire station he can see that other cars are arriving in a hurry as well. Both the station doors are open. They will need a lot of men to fill both fire engines. He parks the car and runs into the station as fast as he can, grabs his boots, his fireman's cloak and his big yellow hat. He can't get on the engine without them. He jumps up on the big red engine. Its great big engines are already roaring. The smoke from the diesel fills the room and smells. The engine is full of men, the doors shut, and off it goes with its blue lights flashing. Sometimes they put the sirens on, but at night the roads are empty so they don't need to. Inside the red engine the men bump together as they put their big coats and hats on but they don't mind. From my bed I can hear the fire engines go up the hill. Nothing sounds the same as these engines. I can see the blue lights flashing in the dark. I get excited and can't get back to sleep. I imagine what's happening, and hope Dad will be back soon. Mum won't sleep until Dad comes home. She always worries about him, so I go in to see her. She gives me a big hug, and I drop off to sleep in Mum's bed.

Back in the engine the men are dressed and on the way. It is probably just another false alarm, most of the calls are, late at night. In the distance they see the glow of a fire. The engines go as fast as they can. This is serious. The two fire engines arrive together. The person in charge can see that they need more help so he gets help on the radio. The men get to work. They quickly roll out the hoses and get gallons and gallons of water shooting into the red hot fire. More of the men get the big ladders out and carry them to the burning house. They need to get some men inside because they think someone is inside. They put on masks and their air tanks so they can breathe inside the thick smoke. You can't believe how hot it is inside. Who would want to go inside a red hot house. But they go straight in, no messing around! There are flames and sparks going everywhere. The water is making a lot of steam and hot water falls back down. The water hisses as it hits the flames. The glass is breaking and bits of the house are falling. The engine pumps are making a lot of noise, the fire roars like a steam train and everyone is busy. The men inside search and search. Then they find the very frightened little boy who is hiding because he didn't know what to do. He is coughing a lot, the firemen give him some clean air and he feels much better. Then quickly, back the way they came to safety. This takes a lot of work in the hot house because the men are tired and they feel like they want to give up but they keep going because if they stop they could all die. They help each other and escape. The fire is nearly out but the big house is ruined. But the little boy is glad that the firemen were brave enough to save him and his mum cries because she is glad too. The firemen are happy and pleased they did everything they could.

Dad comes home, tired and smoky. I'm glad he's safe and I sit down while he has a cup of tea and tells me all about it. One day I will be a fireman like my Dad and then I can jump on the big red engine and save little boys like me. Everyone likes to see the big red engines with the flashing lights, but I smile and say, "My dad could be upon that engine. He's a fireman you know."

I'm proud of my dad!

Rebecca Millar (6)

Sarah Layfield (6)

Lucy Griffin (6)

Emma Catterick (6)

We Are Busy Making a Banner

We are busy making a banner in our class it has got a fringe and it is blue and red and white and we are going to put a gold cross on it and we are going to put some red material on top and it says Darlington Abbey Infants and it has got the first train on it and it is called the Rocket it is a funny name for a train and it has St Cuthberts church on it too. It is a very pretty banner and the cathedral is nine hundred years old that is a very old church it is the oldest. The fringe is made out of wool and the wool is very soft and comfy we will be pilgrims and carry the banner to Durham Cathedral.

Kyle Lawson (6)

Emma Morning (16)

*Dramatic Monologue

Child, I said to her, child, the piano is a musical instrument and a thing of beauty. You must engage your thoughts and feelings, not just the tips of your fingers. That's the problem with young people today; they want everything at the tips of their fingers.

Child, I keep saying, child, if you won't work at it, how can you expect to improve? But then, everything is so instant nowadays. All rash and scurrying, no reflection, no depth. I blame GCSEs and Channel Four, and changes in the weather since the first satellite went up. All we had was the Home Service and the Third Programme – if the reception was good, and the wind was in the right direction.

Child, I said to her, child, when I was a girl, we learnt to pace things and not to cover up difficulties with fancy fingerwork. What was it she said about that scale passage in the Mozart? . . . She said that she had "cocked up". Well really, what sort of language was that for a young lady, and what sort of attitude? When I was a girl, cocks were kept in the farmyard where they belong. Child, I said to her, child, it's a G major scale, can't you see a G major scale? Sometimes I wonder if I'm doing any good.

[PAUSE]

She appears grateful, or rather, her mother does. But you can never tell with those lower classes, especially those with ambition and heavy make-up. What did she say her mother was? A grammar school teacher. Child, I almost said to her, child, when I was a girl, the grammar school teachers worked on our estate to earn extra money, and were grateful.

But she has talent. Child, I said to her last time, child,

with your fingers I could have conquered the world. With your fingers I would not have gone in such fear of them all: Barbarolli, Beecham, and that military Italian, Toscanini. Oh, I had the feeling and the talent, but not the fingers. And now I find the gift in the child of a grammar school teacher. I blame Channel Four.

Child, I say to her, child, it's music, not a race with hob-nailed boots. You must play with feeling. The piano is a musical instrument and a thing of beauty.

Camilla McAuley (9)

*I Feel Sore

In the splits for five seconds
I feel like an old woman
who's walked a mile.
I am slipping down.

In the splits for ten seconds,
She's telling us to bend our legs up at the back.
I can reach my head,
Camilla, Camilla, dear girl, wake up,
you've reached your head.
What?

Emma Williams (14)

The Carpenter

For my Grandad

The man stands,
Hunched over the bench in front of him,
His brow furrowed with thought and concentration.

The wood in front of him lies listlessly,
Unshaped, uncoloured,
Unrecognizable . . .
Waiting to be formed.

He saws slowly and firmly.
The cold metal teeth sink into the wood.
The forming dust
Is blown to the floor,
Before it has a chance to exist.

The room is full of scents and smells,
Like an oriental spice bazaar.
The floor, littered with sawdust, that
Smells fresh and new;
The varnish pot, leaking strange odours
Across the room;
The hot smell of metal on wood,
And the smell of perspiration from the man.
His rough hands sense the grain of the wood,
As it runs in curved patterns
Across the surface.

The plane, gliding along the wood,
Leaves a trail of golden curls behind.
The hands gently brush them away,
And they sink to the floor
Where they are crumpled to dust
Underfoot.

The hands grasping the sandpaper
Rub slowly around the sides:
Ironing out creases,
And smoothing out wrinkles.

The man stands,
Patiently waiting,
As the varnish dries in the warm, spring sunshine.

Patiently, he stands,
Regarding his work with pride.
The soft colours seem to radiate
A soft warmth about the room.

He smiles.

Jessie Binns (16)

**The Workshop

A certain smell
of wood and glue,
of dust and stain and polish,
Wraps itself around the clamps and files
and metal-tasting blades.

The slinking coils of silver wire
glisten secretively in the sun,
and the mottled gut of a broken double-bass string
quietly hugs its white flecks inside itself
like prehistoric flies in resin.

A certain dryness pervades this place,
and a sense of tension released.
Balding bows, let slack and hanging silent.
The cello, with its dislocated neck
and head with scrolls waiting, like some ghastly
Spoil of the Thermopylae,
on the bench beside its shoulder.

The violins hang on the wall
like so many noseless faces,
Stripped of strings and tailpieces
by sticky-fingered children.
They hang upside-down like hens
that have been plucked
And wait in their own dust to be roasted,

And the smell of hot glue and amber rosin
is engrained in everything.
Inside the woody scented womb
The very body vibrates and responds;
It sings with the strings
And keens with the agonized arch of the bow
A song in answer to the trees.

Zoë Brigley (13)

*The Poetry Magician, My Mum

She's the director, the head, the boss,
Although her toast is burnt
And baked beans lumpy
As mushy swamp water.
She sits in her favourite chair,
And holds you with the glittering
Blue eyes of the Ancient Mariner.
Peering through the gold rings of intelligence,
Balanced on a small snub nose
Above two pink lips,
Which took us to different worlds,
From that old pink sofa.
I was there when the Highwayman
Met his grizzly end,
When the Ancient Mariner
Was telling his story,
When Laura went to the Goblin Market
And the Lady of Shalott's
Magic mirror finally cracked.
This character in patchwork coat
Red shoes and long coloured scarf,
Would entwine me in all these stories.
She who doted over her old films
And *film noir* books.
She gave me the confidence
To walk the high wire.

Zoë Brigley (14)

SCHOOL PRIZE WINNERS

Three schools were awarded a School Special Award of £300 for submitting work of outstanding quality:

Channing School, The Bank, Highgate, London N6
Millstrand Integrated School, Portrush, Northern Ireland
Royal Grammar School, Newcastle-upon-Tyne

The following schools won School Awards of £150 for submitting work of the most consistent merit:

Askwith CP School, Askwith, North Yorkshire
Budehaven Community School, Bude, Cornwall
Burnham Grammar School, Burnham, Bucks
Charters School, Sunningdale, Berkshire
Cumnor House School, Haywards Heath, West Sussex
Debenham High School, Debenham, Stowmarket, Suffolk
Ellen Wilkinson High School, Hyde Road, Manchester
Foston CE Junior School, York, North Yorkshire
The Glasgow Academy, Glasgow
Guildford High School, Guildford, Surrey
Halesworth Middle School, Halesworth, Suffolk
Handford Hall Primary School, Ipswich, Suffolk
Highlands Junior School, Ilford, Essex
James Allen's Girls' School, East Dulwich Grove, London SE22
Junior King's School, Canterbury, Kent

Kingsbury Hill House, Marlborough, Wiltshire
The London Oratory School, Seagrave Road, London SW6
Money Darragh Primary School, Annalong, Co Down, Northern Ireland
Newcastle-under-Lyme School, Newcastle, Staffs
The Park School, Dartington, Totnes, Devon
Perranporth School, Perranporth, Cornwall
Port Regis School, Shaftesbury, Dorset
Risby CEVP School, Risby, Bury St Edmunds, Suffolk
Stroud High School, Stroud, Gloucester
Tregelles the Mount School, Dalton Terrace, York
Ursuline Convent High School, Brentwood, Essex
William Farr Comprehensive School, Welton, Lincs

INDEX

* **Award winners**
** **Special award winners**
Illustrators

Catterick, Emma Abbey County Infants' School, Darlington, Co Durham 235
Chaces, Florence Burnham Market Primary School, King's Lynn, Norfolk 177
Charlton, Emma Truro High School for Girls, Truro, Cornwall 192
Coffey, Ellen Handford Hall CP School, Ipswich 177, 208
Cruikshank, *Henry Kilchuimen Academy, Fort Augustus, Inverness 161, 221*
Crush, Barnaby St Mary's Junior School, Faversham, Kent 16
Cullen, *Zoë Perse School for Girls, Cambridge 118*

* **Densham**, Oliver Halesworth Middle School, Halesworth, Suffolk 82
* **Doshi**, Nisha Tregelles The Mount School, York 180, 210, 222
Dryer, *Ben Bishop Wordsworth's School, Salisbury, Wiltshire 184*

Elliot, *Freya St Paul's Girls' School, Brook Green, London 191*

Falvey, *Francis Burnham Market County Primary School, King's Lynn, Norfolk 176*
* **Finnemore**, John Poole Grammar School, Poole, Dorset 26, 166
Forbes Robertson, James Beeston Hall, Cromer, Norfolk 79
Frank, Andrew Foston CE Primary School, Foston York 212, 213
Franks, Eleanor Perse School for Girls, Cambridge 49
* **Friend**, Sylvan Park School, Totnes, Devon 85
Furneaux, John St Nicholas C of E School, Sidmouth 172

** **George**, Amanda Great Cornard Upper School, Sudbury, Suffolk 90
* **Gillo**, Sally Park School, Totnes, Devon 188, 223
Gold, *William Beeston Hall, Cromer, Norfolk 78*
Goodall, *Sarah Foston CE Primary School, Foston, York 122*
* **Gray**, Jemma Port Regis School, Shaftesbury, Dorset 194
Green, Haleana Handford Hall CP School, Ipswich, Suffolk 196